SALLY DALZELL

THE
COMPLETE
CAE

CERTIFICATE IN ADVANCED ENGLISH

COURSE

HEINEMANN

Heinemann International
A division of Heinemann Publishers (Oxford) Ltd
Halley Court, Jordan Hill, Oxford OX2 8EJ

OXFORD LONDON EDINBURGH MADRID PARIS ATHENS
BOLOGNA MELBOURNE SYDNEY AUCKLAND SINGAPORE
TOKYO IBADAN NAIROBI GABORONE HARARE
PORTSMOUTH (NH)

ISBN 0 435 294768
© Sally Dalzell
First published 1993

Printed and bound in Scotland by Cambus Litho

93 94 95 96 10 9 8 7 6 5 4 3 2 1

Author's acknowledgements

Firstly, my thanks go to the Heinemann International editorial and design team who worked on
the project. I am especially grateful to all my friends, relatives, trainees and colleagues who lent their
voices and thoughts to so much of the listening material, in particular to Bruce Goodwin, Alison
Dixon, Rita Fernandez, Sean Byrne, Barry Freeman, and Jeremy de Kerdel. Special thanks for all
the work and assistance are due to Mrs Connie Mark; to the staff and pupils of the New Furness
Primary School; to Ian Edgar for some texts; and to Monty Ashford. I would like to thank all my
colleagues at Hammersmith West London College, particularly John Smith and the Teacher Training
team. Most importantly thanks to those who had to put up with me and the writing throughout:
Frankie, Elisa, Steven and most recently Gemma.

Acknowledgements

The author and publisher would like to thank Judith Ash, Mark Bartram, Liz Hunter and Alan Dury.
The publishers would like to thank the following for their kind permission for use of text: Katie
Campbell for *Gift of the Gab*, p8; Harper Collins Publishers Limited/Unwin Hyman for extract from
Maps and Their Makers by GJ Crone 1966, p118; Maureen Connett for adapted text from *The Master*,
pp21-23; De Agostini Rights Ltd for *The Phantom Face*, p101, *Inside a Black Hole*, p85; Andre
Deutsch Ltd for *Myself with Others* by Carlos Fuentes, p28, *Crick Crack Monkey* by Merle Hodge,
p153, p155; Food & Wine from France Limited for *French Granny Smith* text, p16; The Guardian for
Beyond the frontier spirit, p65, *Car traffic extracts*, p66, and The Guardian/Elizabeth Garrett
Anderson for *Female Victory Against Male Odds*, p32; Julia Hagedorn for *First class to New York*,
pp161-163; Roy Hattersley for *Endpiece*, p55; H&C Communications/Jessica Catto for questionnaire,
p137; HMSO/Sir Ernest Gower for *The Complete Plain Words*, Crown Copyright, p15; The
Independent/Sean O'Neill for *Teenagers strangely happy with their lot*, p44, Louise Hidalgo for
Problem parents and how to deal with them, p50, *Coo Fancy that*, p70, Imogen Edwards-Jones for *A
voyage of no return*, p71, Jamie Donald for *…As mutant vegetables appear near the Russian nuclear
disaster*, p80, *Freak weather in Florida —it's almost scary*, p80, Annabel Maclver for *Can polar bears
tread water*, p80, *Ultrasonic gun 'nobbles' winning racehorse* text and artwork, p88, *Some paranormal
phenomena defined*, p93, doctors' comments and teenagers' comments, p94, extracts from the
levitation experiment, p94, twins text, p104, p168, p173, *Moulting girl*, p111, Martin O'Brien for
Beware the killer jellyfish text , p125, and Helen Brown for *Rabid bats out of hell*, p134; London
News Service/News of the World for *Inga's attraction*, p93, and *Dog leaves owner pegless*, p111;
Longman Dictionaries, for dictionary extracts, p3, and modification of Roget's Thesaurus preface
from Longman 1982, p2; Robert MacNeil for *Wordstruck: A Memoir* by Robert MacNeil, copyright
©1989 by Neely Productions Ltd. Used by permission of Viking Penguin, a division of Penguin
Books USA Inc. for Canada and open market rights, and Faber & Faber Ltd., for world rights
excluding USA, p14; Carol Mann Agency/ Marita Golden for extracts from *Migrations of the Heart*,
p27; The National Magazine Co Ltd and Cosmopolitan (UK Edition) for *What on earth do you see in
those friends* by Linda Franklin, p42, and Cosmopolitan (UK Edition) for *Why some friendships have
to fade*, by Irma Kurtz, p48, Cosmopolitan (UK Edition) for book reviews, p116; Chris Nuttall for
World's smallest islands fear floods from global warming, p80; The Observer for *Discovering friends in
deep places*, p131, Robin McKie for *Hey, diddle diddle —the cow jumped over the Amazon*, p130, and
Luke Blair for *Silvery fish on a line*, p59; Octopus Publishing Group/John Cleese and Robin Skynner
for *Families and how to survive them*, p37; *Amerindians* by permission of Oxford University Press, an
extract from the Oxford Illustrated Encyclopaedia of World History Volume 3, p106, use of the
excerpt *'epigram'* from Oxford Advanced Learner's Dictionary, p11; Peters Fraser & Dunlop Group
Ltd for 4 quotes from *Complete Verse by Hilaire Belloc*, p11; Edward Pilkington for *All stops to hell*,
p53; Random Century Group/Executors of the James Joyce Estate, The Bodley Head for text from
Ulysses by James Joyce, adapted, p5; Reuters Limited for *Babies in fjord live with luck after crash*,
p103, *Everest clean up climb*, p80, and *On the hop*, p129; Rex Features/ Amanda Cable for *10 clues to
help crack secret of the corn circles*, p100, space fans text, p111, *Raiders,70, in an old-up!*, p111, *Thief
roars off in Porsche*, p111; Rogers, Coleridge & White Ltd for excerpts from *Women of our Century*
by Leonie Caldecott, published by BBC 1984, p28; Routledge/Bertrand Russell for excerpts from
postscripts of *What I have lived for*, p145; Christina Ruse and Elana Katz for excerpts of *fate, chance,
and coincidence* from the Heinemann International Students Dictionary, p102; Walter Schwarz for
Small, but beautiful, p84; Paul Simons for *Spider grabs, Behaviour*, p132; Jonathan Steele for *Russians
'sight alien beings'* as appeared in The Guardian, p98; Michael Symons for extracts from *One
Continuous Picnic: A history of eating in Australia*, Adelaide: Duck Press, 1982, p18; Nick Vandome
for *Goodbye high school, hello Africa*, pp161-163, Virago Press/Margaret Atwood for *Introduction to
Margaret Atwood*, p34; Robert Walgate for *A long hop*, p122.

Illustrations by: Terry Aldridge p101; John Bishop/Maggie Mundy Agency p13, p79; p107;
David Brancaleone p17; Richard Buckley/Maggie Mundy Agency p69; Ann Gowland pp24-25, p151;
Hardlines p78, p79, p121, p169, p172; Ian Kellas p1, p39, p93, p104, p135, p148.

Photographs by: Aspect Picture Library Ltd, p75, p147; BBC Photograph Library, p20; Sue Baker,
p169, p171, p154; Bridgeman Art Library, p21; Camera Press Ltd, p150; The Cinema Museum, p97;
Bruce Coleman Ltd, p63; Float Systems International, p87; Paul Freestone, p92; Sally and Richard
Greenhill, p150, p152, p171, p172; The Hulton/Deutsch Collection, p35; The Hutchison Library,
p171; The Image Bank, p150; Impact Photos Ltd, p52, p147; The Independent, p126; The
International Stock Exchange Photo Library, p79; Frank Lane Picture Agency Ltd, p75, p129, p137;
Mander & Mitchenson Theatre Collection, p5; Connie Mark, p143; NHPA, p7, p79, p123; Oxford
Scientific Films Ltd Photo Library, p121, p131, p132, p137; Franta Provaznik, p27; Rex Features Ltd,
p138; Science Photo Library Ltd, p71, p92; Jim Selby/ Vista, p121; South American Pictures, p171;
Tony Stone Worldwide Photolibrary, p52; The Vintage Magazine Company, p37, p97, p154.

Cassettes produced by Liz Hunter.

INTRODUCTION

The Complete CAE Course prepares you for the Certificate in Advanced English examination in two ways: by developing your standard of English to a genuine advanced level, and by developing particular skills necessary for the examination. You can also use this course if you are an upper intermediate student who wishes to progress to an advanced level whether or not you intend to take the examination.

Organisation

The course is organised into 10 Themes, each containing three units, and one Exam Section. Within each unit material is organised into sections. The number of sections and content of each section is unique to allow for the most appropriate exploitation of the material. Exam Sections contain on average three questions, presented in exam format.

A Grammar Review is included at the end of the book.

The Certificate in Advanced English

There are five papers in the examination: 1 Reading 2 Writing 3 English in Use 4 Listening 5 Speaking

Each Paper is worth 20% and the marks are totalled to give an overall grade.

Paper 1 Reading (1 hour)

This consists of four questions testing a range of reading skills and strategies. You must answer all four questions.

Paper 2 Writing (2 hours)

This paper is divided into two sections. Section A is compulsory and consists of a writing task based on the reading and analysis of texts. In Section B you can choose from four different writing activities. Each piece of writing should be approximately 250 words.

Paper 3 English in Use (1 hour 30 minutes)

This paper is divided into three sections. Section A consists of two gap filling exercises. The first focuses on lexical items and the second on grammatical items. Section B focuses on the identification of errors and inappropriacies of various kinds (spelling, punctuation, style). Section C consists of completing a text or constructing a text from notes of various kinds.

Paper 4 Listening (approx. 45 minutes)

This paper is divided into four sections, usually containing one text per section. All pieces are heard twice, except for Section B where it is heard only once. Section A and B test understanding of informational language; Section C and D test understanding of identification of context, gist and attitude and interpretation.

Paper 5 Speaking (15 minutes)

Candidates are examined in pairs by two examiners. There are four Phases. Phase A tests social and interactional language; Phase B tests transactional language; Phase C tests negotiation and collaboration skills, and Phase D tests reporting and summarising skills.

As you work through the course you will find more detailed explanations of the papers and the questions. Strategies to help you with the exam are also included.

CONTENTS

Listening	Speaking	Pronunciation	Exam section
Identifying words	Discussing meaning		English in Use Section A - vocabulary multiple choice English in Use Section B - proof reading for errors
Identifying meaning Gist	Expressing likes/dislikes Describing feelings	Nuclear stress Information chunks	
Gist Identifying words		Nuclear stress and rhythm Rhyming words	
Note taking	Speculating		Reading multiple choice English in Use Section B – proof reading for missing words Listening Section D – match ranking Writing Section B
True/false Text completion	Giving opinion Describing		
Matching – descriptions – topic and tone	Speculating Describing Talks		
Connotation Gist Identifying relationships and mood/tone	Speculating Giving opinion Expressing annoyance Relating a plot		English in Use Section B – proof reading for extra words English in Use Section C – constructing text from notes Reading multiple match Writing Section B Speaking Phase A
Multiple match Interpreting context and tone	Negotiating Justifying Describing relationships	Information chunks Nuclear stress and rhythm	
Checking predictions	Negotiating Describing Agreeing/disagreeing		
For facts Descriptions	Speculating Describing Recounting		Listening Section A – completing facts Speaking Phase C/D
Note taking	Analysing differences Describing Negotiating		
Note taking	Predicting Commenting Debating		
	Expressing beliefs and doubts Negotiating		English in Use Section A – vocabulary multiple choice English in Use Section B – register rewriting Reading Gapped text
Text completion Note taking Labelling/completing diagrams	Expressing beliefs and giving opinions Talks Exchanging information	Intonation	
For confirmation True/false	Justifying Negotiating		

CONTENTS

Listening	Speaking	Pronunciation	Exam section
Correcting information Grid completion	Speculating Hypothesising Expressing likelihood	Intonation	English in Use Section C – gapped text Speaking Phase B English in Use Section B – proof reading for missing words
Note taking Matching	Agreeing/disagreeing Reporting Recounting an experience		
	Speculating Expressing likelihood Interviews	Intonation Nuclear stress	
Note taking	Analysing Relating a story		Reading multiple match Listening Section D – match ranking English in Use Section C – gapped text
Correcting information Note taking Confirming facts	Giving opinion Reporting Speculating Asking for confirmation Exchanging information	Intonation for confirmation	
Summarising	Summarising Relating anecdotes		
Matching topic and tone	Speculating Persuading Exchanging information	Relating stress and meaning	English in Use Section A – gap filling Writing Section B Speaking Phase C
Text completion	Reacting Exclaiming Talks		
Identifying Topic and purpose	Exchanging information	Intonation Sentence stress and given/new information	
Multiple match Interpreting contexts Grid completion	Expressing preference and tastes Interviewing		Speaking Phase A, Phase B, Phase C, Phase D
True/false	Speculating Past preferences Talks		
Note taking	Describing Expressing beliefs Analysing and interpreting		
Note taking Extracting facts Giving personal response	Giving opinions Comparing Expressing past expectations	Information chunks and stress	Writing Section A English in Use Section C – constructing text from notes Listening Section D – multiple match
Grid completion Text completion from notes	Describing Expressing wishes and regrets		
Interpreting tone and topic	Negotiating Predicting Assessing proposals		

THE MEANING 1

1 Discuss
Read this well-known English saying. Discuss exactly what it means. In your opinion is this true or not? Explain why.

2 Vocabulary
a All languages have idioms or expressions which use 'word' or 'words'. Think of some in your language. Explain both the literal meaning and the real meaning of the expressions to the class.

b Match these English expressions using 'word' with their meaning in the list.

c Select the appropriate idiom and complete these sentences, making the necessary changes.

Sticks and stones can break your bones but words can never harm you.

Idioms	Meanings
• to have a way with words	• sensible, intelligent remarks
• word for word	• verbal repetition of something with no errors
• a word of warning	• they must be obeyed
• words fail somebody	• to be able to express ideas very well
• somebody's word is law	• they cannot think of what to say
• to be word perfect	• exactly as in the original
• words of wisdom	• a piece of advice about some danger

1 _____ her as she looked around at the scene of devastation.

2 The children must be _____ for the poetry recital.

3 If she does not like it you won't be able to do anything; her _____ in this office.

4 Given the political tension the _____ she uttered were welcomed by all.

5 'Copy that out again _____ ,' said the teacher.

6 'Let me give you _____ . Don't let your ambitions cloud your judgement.'

7 One of my favourite authors is James Joyce; he really _____

Section   B

1 Read

a Skim read the passage and answer these questions.
 1 What are the contents of this Thesaurus?
 2 Why is this book a useful accompaniment to a dictionary?

b Scan the text. How long does it take you to find:
 1 the title of a section?
 2 the reason why you can find the best word for your purpose?
 3 the meaning of 'thesaurus'?
 4 the types of words found with the same meaning?
 5 the number of 'classes' in the book?

Dr Mark Roget first published his *Thesaurus of English Words and Phrases* over 130 years ago but it is equally valued today as it was by preceding generations. 'Thesaurus' means treasury or storehouse and *Roget's Thesaurus* is a storehouse of the English language, collecting together words and phrases of every possible kind; from the formal to the colloquial, from poetic and old-fashioned to modern slang; it draws from all areas from art, literature, history and modern society. All the expressions and words are sorted into groups of related meanings with headings such as Duty, Speech, Darkness. Groups follow a logical sequence within a section and these sections fall within a 'class' of which there are only six. For example, the sections *Space in General, Dimensions, Form, Motion* are all classified under Class 2, *Space*.

The *Thesaurus* is a valuable complement to a Dictionary. While a dictionary gives the meaning of a particular word, the *Thesaurus* offers a variety of different words with which to express a given meaning. You cannot find a word which you have forgotten or do not know in a dictionary because you cannot look it up without knowing the spelling. But if you look up a word of similar meaning in the *Thesaurus*, you will discover a variety of expressions which probably include the one at the back of your mind or you will find ones which are unknown to you and which you can then look up in a dictionary. So the combination of a thesaurus and a dictionary allows you to greatly increase your vocabulary. A cross-referencing system to other groups gives a wider choice.

It is the wide range and diversity of the vocabulary in a thesaurus which allows you to find the most appropriate expression for your purpose. This helps you write better as the act of selecting a word forces you to really consider what you are trying to say. The variety ranging from swear words and everyday expressions to scientific terms all with the same meaning, allows you to express your ideas more appropriately for the situation. But the *Thesaurus* is more than a useful tool for writing (and reading). As a treasure-house of English words and phrases, it can give great pleasure to word-lovers who can simply enjoy browsing through the pages or who need help with a crossword puzzle.

2 Vocabulary

a Look at the following extract from *Roget's Thesaurus*. This is part of the group *Word* in the section *Means of Communicating Ideas* in Class 4, *Intellect*. What do you think is the function of the numbers? Underline the words you know.

559. Word–N. *word*, expression, locution 563 *phrase*; term. vocable 561 *name*; phoneme, syllable; semanteme 514 *meaning*; synonym 13 *identity:* homonym, homograph, homophone; weasel word 518 *equivocalness*; antonym 14 *contrariety*; etymon, root, back-formation; folk etymology; derivation, derivative, paronym, doublet; morpheme, stem, inflection; part of speech 564 *grammar*; diminutive, pejorative, intensive; enclitic abbreviation, acronym, portmanteau word 569 *conciseness*; cliche, catchword, vogue word, buzz w., trigger w.; nonce w., new w., loan w. 560 *neology*; assonant 18 *similarity*; four-letter word 573 *plainness*; swearword 899 *malediction*; hard word, jawbreaker, mouthful; long word, polysyllable; short word, monosyllable; verbosity 570 *pleonasm*.

dictionary, lexicon, wordbook, wordstock, wordlist, glossary, vocabulary; gra

b Choose four words you do not know and look them up in a dictionary. Write an example sentence for each. Explain the words/phrases to two other students.

Section C

1 Listen

a Listen to these definitions of four words by children. Guess the word each time. Be careful, some of the information may not be accurate.

b Listen again. Ask the teacher to stop the tape at any words you do not know. Try to guess the meaning from the context. Use a dictionary if necessary.

2 Task

a Choose six words/phrases and write definitions giving five pieces of information for each. Order your information starting with the most difficult.

b Compete with the class. Take it in turns to give one of your definitions to the rest of the class. Pause briefly after each piece of information. The others try to guess the word as soon as possible. A correct answer scores one point.

Section D

1 Games

Playing word games will increase and improve your vocabulary.

1 Select a long word (for example: definition) and see how many other words (of three or more letters) you can make from it.

2 Choose a topic area (for example: food) and design a small crossword (10-15 words). Write the clues. Then swap crosswords.

3 Hangman. One person thinks of a word and draws a dash for each letter on the board. The class calls out letters. Correct ones are filled in; incorrect ones are listed and a line of the sketch is drawn each time. The complete diagram has 11 lines. If the class does not guess the word before completion of the sketch then they lose and the same person does another word.

a d _ _ a n _ e d

g h i o m r
b t s p l

4 Use a set of Scrabble letters or make a set of alphabet cards (with three examples of each vowel and two examples of the most common consonants: B C D H L M N P R S T Y). Separate the vowels and consonants and mix well. Students work in teams of 4/5. A spokesperson for one team chooses a consonant or a vowel until 10 letters are exposed. All the groups try to make the longest word possible using any of the letters. Time limit: one minute. The group with the longest word scores a point. Each group should have a turn at selecting the letters.

5 Use Scrabble letters or alphabet cards (shuffled) and students in four teams. Lay out nine letters, one in each square (see diagram).

E	B	L
N	A	S
C	H	T

Team 1 makes a word incorporating any three letters in a straight line always using the centre letter. Team 2 makes another but cannot use the same sequence. Only the centre letter can be used more than once and it must be used each time. Score 1 point for each correct word. Teams may pass if they cannot make a word. Continue until all letters are used.

Learner Skills

- finding out the meaning of words
- guessing the meaning of words in context
- losing fear of unknown words
- developing confidence with words
- understanding skimming and scanning as reading strategies
- using reference books
- listening for meaning/focusing on the content
- learning to work with others in pairs/groups

THE FEELING

2

Puck   My fairy Lord, this must be done with haste,

For night's sweet dragons cut the clouds full fast,

And yonder shines Aurora's harbinger;

At whose approach, ghosts, wandering here and there,

Troop home to churchyards: damned spirits all

That in crossways and floods have burial,

Already to their wormy beds are gone;

For fear lest day should look their shames upon,

They willfully themselves exile from light

And must for aye consort with black-brow'd night.

1 Read

Some people have a way with words. Think about the talent of writers such as William Shakespeare or James Joyce.

Skim read these two extracts. Do not worry about understanding but concentrate on the flow of the words. Discuss whether you like them or not. Say why.

2 Pronunciation

Now read more slowly. Read aloud to yourself under your breath.

Underline the syllable/words you stress.

Listen to these pieces read aloud. Are the same words stressed? When we read (aloud or silently) we put the information into chunks and pause between each. Listen again to the extract by Joyce and mark every time there is a pause.

Men, men, men.

Perched on high stools by the bar, hats shoved back, at the tables calling for more bread no charge, swilling, wolfing gobfuls of sloppy food, their eyes bulging, wiping wetted moustaches. A pallid suetfaced young man polished his tumbler knife fork and spoon with his napkin. New set of microbes. A man with an infant's saucestained napkin tucked round him shovelled gurgling soup down his gullet. A man spitting back on his plate: halfmasticated gristle: gums: no teeth to chewchewchew it.

3 Vocabulary

Listen and read the two extracts. Circle any words which you particularly like or dislike. Can you say why? Discuss your feelings about the words in the texts. Check the meaning of your marked words. Do you still feel the same about each word?

4 Language

Compound adjectives

One way to be descriptive in English is by combining words to form compound adjectives. These can be formed by joining:

• two nouns • two adjectives • noun and adjective

a Find examples in both passages and say which they are.

b What feature do the examples in Joyce have in common? This is one of the commonest ways to form compounds from nouns and verbs. Form other compound adjectives using the nouns: *face, hair, eye, shoulder.*

Section B

1 Speak

Do you like words? Are there any words you like or dislike in your language? What about in English? Think of two words/phrases you particularly like in English and two you particularly dislike. Discuss them with the class and see if others agree or disagree with your choices. Explain why.

2 Vocabulary

Find out the meaning of the words in this list.

nice   over the top   squabble

Think of situations in which each word could be used.

3 Listen

a Three people say how they feel about the listed words. Listen and complete the chart numbering the speakers 1 to 3. The first one has been done for you. Asterisk the ones which you agree with.

	Like	Dislike	Neutral	Unclear
nice		*1*		
over the top				
squabble				

Study Tips

Speaking activities   Activities entitled 'speak' are designed to provide controlled practice of particular language items. Make sure you practise using the indicated function/s or structure/s. In this case you should revise all the patterns you know for expressing likes and dislikes.

b The same people give examples of words they particularly like and dislike. Listen and say whether you agree or disagree with them. Respond to the sound if you do not know the meaning. Note all the words and work together to find out the meaning.

Section   C

1 Vocabulary

a Study the photograph. How does it make you feel? Note six words or phrases which describe it positively and six which describe it negatively.

b Discuss your feelings with a partner. Compare the words and phrases you have noted. Do you have similar or different feelings about the photograph?

2 Write

Write a paragraph using all 12 of your words/phrases to describe the place, the atmosphere and your feelings about the photo. Do not write more than 80–100 words. Work in rough first then ask a partner to check for errors. Make any corrections and write a good copy.

Section D

1 Listen

Listen to three short excerpts. What are all the speakers doing? Is this considered a good or a bad thing in your society?

2 Read

a Skim read the text and find out:
  1 if the word *gossip* has always had the same meaning.
  2 if the author considers *gossip* to be a good or a bad thing.
  3 if the author accepts or rejects the present day notion that only women *gossip*.
  4 the meaning of the title.

b Scan the text and find:
  1 the original meaning of the word *gossip*.
  2 who the peasants meant by Mother and Father.
  3 what psychiatrists say they talk about in the evening.
  4 what type of people are supposedly those that gossip.
  5 who said that gossip is more interesting than any other speech.
  6 whose writing would have been less effective without gossip.

Katie Campbell talks talk

Gift of the gab

GOSSIP. I love it. Unashamedly, unrepentingly. Most people do, though few will admit it these days. To gossip: to natter, to prattle, to chatter, to tittle-tattle, to jabber, to jaw. As far back as 700 BC Hesiod was wary of it. "Gossip is mischievous, light and easy to raise, but grievous to bear and hard to get rid of." In other words, mud sticks.

But gossip hasn't always had such bad press. Even Oscar Wilde called it charming — granted he was one of history's great gossipers, but he was an even greater gossipee. It has often been noted that while barbarians fight with hatchets, civilised men fight with gossip. Well, frankly, I'd rather have a little mud than a hatchet thrown at my back. And gossip needn't be malevolent; my Little Oxford Dictionary defines it simply as "informal talk, esp about persons." In any case, when someone gossips well they are called a wit or a conversationalist; only those who gossip badly are tarred with the appellation "Gossip".

The word gossip itself actually means "god's kin". Originally it was a term of respect denoting a godparent — as Queen Elizabeth I was the gossip at the baptism of her godson James VI, or indicating friends with a common spiritual bond. Following the peasant habit of referring to any elder as "Mother / Father" or "Grandmother/Grandfather", the word was also applied to any gathering of older folk. It was only when it began to be associated exclusively with women that gossip began its slippery slide into the gutter. From denoting women friends or gossips, the word came to denote the speech of gossips. And so it acquired its contemporary, pejorative connotation of idle chatter.

There is a theory that gossip is a form of speech particular to women — to women, old people, servants and slaves.

A psychiatrist friend of mine recently returned from an international conference in Athens. When I asked him what those eminent shrinks did with themselves in the evenings he explained that they gathered in the hotel bar. "And what did you all talk about?"

"Shop-talk: who's getting ahead, and how, and why; who's feuding with whom;

ho's working with whom."

'Oh, you mean gossip."

'No!" he protested, in-
dignantly. "We were talking
hop; it was shop-talk, not
ossip."

When academics delve into
omeone's life it is called
iography; when therapists
osit theories on human
ehaviour it is called Psy-
nology; when sociologists
minate on society it is called
ociology. When women ponder
n an individual, emotion or
cial phenomenon, it is called
ossip.

So what exactly is gossip —
is thing that is so reviled and
ondemned? Gossip is Spec-
lation. About human affairs,
bout human motives, actions
nd desires. As women are
argely responsible for the
motional wellbeing of society,
is hardly surprising that the
nop-talk of women is gossip.

Gossip is Old Wives' Tales.
Vomen's wisdom has long been
eared: Old Women, Witches,
ibyls, Seers. Those who scorn
r censure women's talk
iminish women. Or seek to.

In short, gossip is a chronicle
f humanity. As Ogden Nash put
, "Another good thing about
ossip is that it is within
verybody's reach/And it is
uch more interesting than any
ther form of speech ..."

Imagine if Colette or Jane
usten or Dorothy Parker or
haucer or Shakespeare or
Marcel Proust had lived in a
orld without gossip! Their
orks would be skeletal; their
nsights would be meagre and
ean. You can keep your
hilosophers speculating on
anguage or your theologians
peculating on God, I'll
peculate on the human heart
– gossip's good enough for me.

3 Vocabulary

It is possible to guess the meaning of unknown words
from grammatical knowledge and the context.

For example, from paragraph one what does *to tittle
tattle* mean? Why/how do you know? If you had seen
the word in isolation it would have had no meaning for
you.

Work through the text applying logic, word building
skills, and knowledge of other languages to help you
guess the meaning (or the approximate meaning) of the
following words in the text.

>hatchet   denoting   pejorative
>shrinks   delve   skeletal

4 Language

Tense review

a Find the following examples in the text:

Simple Present
my Little Oxford Dictionary defines ...

Present Continuous
who's getting ahead ...

Simple Past
When I asked him ...

Present Perfect
gossip hasn't always had a ...

Past Continuous
We were talking shop ...

Past Perfect
Imagine if ... Proust had lived in ...

Now find other examples of each tense. Go over
your examples and say why each particular tense is
used in each case.

That's most of my news — I suppose you'd like to hear news of some of the others who were on the course. Well, I know that Paul *has got a* really nice job in Paris and Sue _____ there looking for work — I wonder if they _____ together! Pam, as you know, is pregnant but _____ at the Institute though she may only go back to part-time work after the birth. Janet _____ Peru last month but _____ from her yet. Simon _____ opposite me right now and sends you his love — he said he was going to add something to this letter, I'll wait and see. And that's all the gossip I've got. What about John? _____ him when you were in Tokyo? Did you have a good time? How long _____ there? I _____ to have received those books _____ but I _____ the post is very slow. I'm sure they'll arrive soon. Thanks for sending them anyway and _____ yourself. Write soon.

Lots of love Angie.

b Complete this letter (between friends) with any appropriate word/s. Be particularly careful about the tenses you use.

Learner Skills

- exploring feelings about words
- listening for nuclear stress and information chunks
- developing confidence in handling unknown words
- guessing meaning in context
- listening for gist meaning
- developing skimming and scanning skills

Exam Skills

Listening
B3a identifying speakers and matching

Speaking
C1 interpreting a photograph

Writing
C2 descriptive writing

English in Use
D4b completing a text

THE SOUND

3

epigram /ˈepigræm/ n short poem or saying expressing an idea in a clever and amusing way.

Oxford Advanced Learner's Dictionary

1 Read

The poet Hillaire Belloc (1870–1953) was a master at writing epigrams. Note that the use of capital letters is very different from the way we use them today.

Read and listen simultaneously. Say:
a if Belloc led a very moral life.
b if Norman was well liked.
c in what kind of place was the dog buried.
d if Belloc respected the politician.

2 Pronunciation

a Practise reading the poems aloud. Underline the words you think are stressed. Listen again and check your work.

b In *On his books* the two words said /sed/ and read /red/ rhyme perfectly but are spelt differently. Listen again and find other examples.

c Think of another five pairs of rhyming words and compile a class list.

3 Vocabulary

a Find the word/s in the epigrams which mean:
a dead body, to speak badly of someone, a red colour, to want very much.

b The verb *to strike* is used here to mean *an idea strikes you*. In what other situations can you use this verb? Give examples.

On his books
When I am dead I hope it may be said:
'His sins were scarlet, but his books were read.'

On Norman, a Guest
Dear Mr Norman,
does it ever strike you,
The more we see of you,
the less we like you.

Epitaph on Favourite dog of a politician
Here lies a Dog: may every Dog that dies
Lie in security — as this Dog lies.

Epitaph on the Politician Himself
Here richly, with ridiculous display,
The politician's corpse
was laid away.
While all of his acquaintance sneered and slanged
I wept: for I had longed to see him hanged.

Study Tips

Collocation   Certain words combine with other words: this is called collocation. In many cases the combination of words will be different in your first language. For example: in English you *sit / take / have / do* an examination but in some languages the verb is make. What do you say in your language? It is important to note collocations in your vocabulary notebook.

4 Language
Comparison
a Study this sentence:
The more we see of you the less we like you.
Complete this sentence to give another example:
The less we … the more we … .

b We can use other adjectives/adverbs in the comparative form in this way. The adjectives/adverbs may be opposites (as above) but they do not have to be.
The harder you work the more you achieve.
The subject of both clauses can be the same or different:
The faster you drive the louder he screams.

c Write examples using each of the following in initial position:
the better	*the more violent*	*the easier*
the sooner	*the more ridiculous*	*the worse*
the happier	*the quicker*	

Clause of reason — *for*
a In the epigram *Epitaph on the Politician Himself* look at the last line. Did the poet cry? Why/why not?
Look back at the Shakespeare text and find a similar example using *for*. What word can be substituted for *for* in both texts? Which of these words is most often used to introduce a clause of reason?

b Write example sentences (with clauses of reason) on the board. Discuss with the teacher whether both words can be used in each case.

Section B

1 Write
Step 1 Choose one of the following topics:
Granny   My Teacher   Babies   Wine   Education
The President   The Railways   Space   Breakfast

Step 2 Note down all the words you can think of which relate to the topic.

Step 3 Identify any words which rhyme.

Step 4 Put together two or three sentences, each ending with a rhyming word. Try to use at least one example of the comparative pattern above.

2 Pronunciation
Mark the stressed words in your epigrams. Read them aloud to the class. Stick them on the wall. Go round and read them.

Section C

1 Listen

Nursery rhymes are often the first songs and poems which small children learn. Some of them are very old and have been passed down from generation to generation.

a Listen to these four and match them to the pictures.

b Listen again. Some rhyming words are missing. Try to think of suitable words which will fit the rhyme.

c Make a note of each rhyming pair.

Learner Skills

- finding information in a text
- developing awareness of English stress and rhythm
- developing awareness of collocation
- listening to understand context
- listening intensively

Exam Skills

Reading
A1 extracting facts from text

Listening
C identifying context

EXAM SECTION

Read the article below and circle the letter next to the word which best fits each space. The first answer has been given as an example.

Broadcasting has democratized the publication of language, often at its most informal, even undressed. Now the ears of the educated cannot escape the language of the masses. It (1) … them on the news, weather, sports, commercials, and the ever-proliferating game shows.

This wider dissemination of popular speech may easily give purists the (2) … that language is suddenly going to hell in this generation, and may (3) … the new paranoia about it.

It might also be argued that more Americans hear more correct, even beautiful, English on television than ever before. Through television more models of good usage (4) … more American homes than was ever possible in other times. Television gives them lots of (5) … English too, some awful, some creative, but that is not new.

Hidden in this is a (6) … fact: our language is not the special private property of the language police, or grammarians, or teachers, or even great writers. The (7) … of English is that it has always been the tongue of the common people, literate or not.

English belongs to everybody: the funny (8) … of phrase that pops into the mind of a farmer telling a story; or the (9) … salesman's dirty joke; or the teenager saying, 'Gag me with a spoon'; or the pop lyric — all contribute, are all as (10) … as the tortured image of the academic, or the line the poet sweats over for a week.

Through our collective language (11) … some may be thought beautiful and some ugly, some may live and some may die: but it is all English and it (12) … to everyone — to those of us who wish to be careful with it and those who don't care.

Exam Strategies

Vocabulary multiple choice — English in Use. For each gap in the text you are given four possible words to choose from. Procedure: skim read the complete text. Some words may come to mind immediately, note them (and the number) on scrap paper. Take each idea you had and look at the options to see if one matches your idea. This way you can fill some gaps. Go through the remainder one by one reading the surrounding text. Think of your own idea before looking at the options and eliminate the options. Move on if you are having difficulty. Gradually fill in more gaps each time you read through the text.

	a		b		c		d	
1	a	circles	b	surrenders	c	supports	**d**	surrounds
2	a	thought	b	idea	c	sight	d	belief
3	a	justify	b	inflate	c	explain	d	idealise
4	a	render	b	reach	c	expose	d	leave
5	a	colloquial	b	current	c	common	d	spoken
6	a	central	b	stupid	c	common	d	simple
7	a	genii	b	genius	c	giant	d	generalisation
8	a	turn	b	twist	c	use	d	time
9	a	tour	b	transport	c	travel	d	travelling
10	a	valued	b	valid	c	truthful	d	imperfect
11	a	sense	b	structure	c	ideas	d	senses
12	a	caters	b	concerns	c	belongs	d	communicates

ENGLISH IN USE   Section B

In most lines of the following text there is an error. It is either grammatically incorrect or there is a word which does not fit the sense of the text. Read the text, put a line through each error and then write the correct version in the space provided at the end of the line. Some lines are correct. Indicate these lines with a tick against the line number. The first two lines have been done.

The Choice of Words: introductory

1	Here we comes to the most important part of our subject. Correctness is	_come_ 1
2	not enough. The words used may all be words approved by the dictionary	✓ 2
3	and used in their right senses; the grammar may be faultful and the	_____ 3
4	idiom above reproach. Yet what is written may yet fail to convey a	_____ 4
5	ready and precise meaning at the reader. This failure is the weakness of	_____ 5
6	much of what was written nowadays, including much of what is written by	_____ 6
7	officials. Matthew Arnold once says that the secret of style was to have	_____ 7
8	something to say and to say it as clearly as you can. This is over-simple	_____ 8
9	but it will done as a first principle for the kind of writing in which	_____ 9
10	emotional appeal plays no part. The more prevalent disease in present-	_____ 10
11	day writing is a tendency to say what you has to say in as complicated a	_____ 11
12	way as possible. Instead to being simple, and direct, it is stilted, and	_____ 12
13	long-winded; instead of choose the simple word it prefers the unusual;	_____ 13
14	instead of that plain phrase the cliche.	_____ 14

THEIR LIVES

4

1 Read

a Skim this text. What is it? Where could you see it? What are Granny Smiths?

b Scan the text and find an example of comparison and an example of humour. Exchange your examples with the class.

2 Vocabulary

Humour is shown here with double meaning for some phrases. What are the two meanings for each of the following?
Granny Smiths (line 4)   *hang around in the sun* (line 6)
it comes to 'Le Crunch' (line 15)
your Grannies (line 20)
you now know exactly which ones to pick (line 22)

Write example sentences for *to hang around* and *to come to the crunch*.

3 Language
Comparison
Comparison is often used for description.

a There are six examples of comparison used to describe the item in the advert. Underline and number them.

b Comparison means comparing one item with another. What two items are compared in examples 1, 3, 4 above?

c Frequently the second item is not specified. It is usually understood by the reader/listener either because of the context or simple logic. What is the second item in 2 and 5?

d Examples 1, 2, 5, 6 are probably patterns you know. Study examples 3 and 4 in the text and below.
  3 *(Just) as sure as x will happen y will happen.*
  (Just) as sure as night will fall, apples will always be eaten.
  4 *... exactly as an x + should/does/might.*
  The girl danced exactly as a ballerina does.

Now write two examples for each pattern.

The French have something healthier than sugar to sweeten their Granny Smiths. Lucky old Granny Smiths. They can hang around in the sun all day, and only good can come of it. Constant sun helps them to become crisp and develop a noticeably sweeter taste. Now in France, just as sure as a cock will crow the sun will rise and shine. Which means that when it comes to 'Le Crunch' French Granny Smiths will always taste exactly as a Granny Smith should. So if you like your Grannies to be deliciously crisp and naturally sweeter, you now know exactly which ones to pick. And that can only be a healthy change for the better.

4 Write

Step 1 Choose a fruit which grows locally. Think of five possible positive comparisons you can make. Arrange them in a suitable order not specifying the second item for at least three of them.

Step 2 Consider if there is any other information you could add to your advert. Can you think of a suitable idiom to introduce double-meaning humour?

Step 3 Now you have the content of the advert write it out in a rough copy. Remember layout and pictures.

Step 4 Re-read the rough copy looking for any errors or improvements. Use reference books to check and only write out a good copy when you think the work is all correct.

Step 5 Exchange your adverts. Are there any errors? Find their comparative examples. Identify their unspecified items.

Section   B

1 Discuss

Look at the picture. Imagine what sort of life this woman had. List six points about her life. Find out if other students agree with you.

Granny Smith died long before her apple became famous and for this reason much of her story is lost. Born Maria Ann Sherwood in the village of Peasemarsh in the South of England, she married
5 Thomas Smith from a nearby town and the couple grew hops for a living. They had had five children by the time they set off aboard the Lady Nugent to emigrate to Australia, arriving in New South Wales in 1838. Eventually they settled on farming
10 land in the Ryde district. Later the three sons all became farmers and the daughters married local fruit farmers. By the time she was in her sixties Maria was widely known as 'Granny'. Her husband was an invalid and 'Granny' used to take the
15 produce from their small orchard to market. One local story says that she, unknowingly, brought home some cases of rotten Tasmanian apples, probably French Crabs. She threw them away among the ferns beside her creek only to find a
20 few years later — probably 1868 — a young seedling bearing a few fine apples. As the tree had grown from a seed it was a cross breed — pollinated from other apple blossom in the vicinity — a new, natural hybrid. It is known that
25 she showed the apples to visitors among them a Mr Small and his twelve-year-old son. Mr Small thought they would make good cooking apples, but his son (who recalled the story in 1924) found the green-skinned apples good for eating.
30 Another version of the story was that a local

fruitmerchant gave 'Granny' some French Crabs to test their cooking quality. She made apple pies, throwing the peel and cores out of the kitchen window, and a seedling grew close to the wall. However, whichever of the stories is true, Granny   35 Smith passed away soon after on March 9 1870 without knowing that the apples would become so famous.

Though the original tree was soon cleaned out, other local growers, including her sons-in-law had   40 started growing the variety and soon most of the fruit farms and orchards in the area were growing 'Granny Smith' trees. By 1895 the NSW Department of Agriculture was recommending them as a late cooking apple suitable for export but in 1904   45 they re-classified it as an eating apple. With the importation of oil wrapping tissues from the USA in the following year and the experiments with cold storage it was found that 'Granny Smiths' picked in March could be stored until November,   50 a tremendous attribute.

Maria Ann Smith received little recognition for her legacy but in 1950 a small local park was named after her. Today forty per cent of all apples grown in Australia are Granny Smiths. Fifty per   55 cent of all apples exported from Australia are Granny Smiths. They are also extensively grown in New Zealand, South Africa, France, Chile, Argentina and the USA.

2 Read

a Skim read the passage and see if any of your guesses were correct.

b Are the following statements true or false?
1 Thomas Smith lived a long way from Maria Sherwood.
2 In England, neither of the Smiths worked.
3 Initially they did not intend to settle in Australia.
4 All their children stayed in farming.
5 Thomas Smith became sick in later years.
6 Maria bought the French Crabs deliberately.
7 A hybrid is a cross-breed of two types of apple tree.
8 Mr Smith and his sons were the only people to see the apple tree in the early days.
9 Maria enjoyed the fame.
10 After a time very few farms grew the apples.
11 Improved packaging allowed the apples to be stored.
12 Maria became a national hero.

Exam Strategies

Statements on a text — Reading. These may be True/False statements. Procedure: skim the statements first. Then skim read the text. Select the most obvious statements and check the text carefully. Note your answers on scrap paper. Read the statements very carefully. Do not jump to conclusions. Find the relevant part in the text and work out the truth. Make a final check on all statements before marking the answer sheet.

c Inference. The answers to these questions are not directly stated in the passage but they can be worked out/understood from the information that is given. In each case say 'how' you know the answer.
1 How many daughters did the Smiths have?
2 In later life (but before the apples) how did the local people consider Maria?
3 Was Maria proud of the apples on her tree?
4 Why would a seedling grow from what Granny threw out the window?

d Reference. What does each of the following items refer to?
1 this reason (line 2)   5 the story (line 30)
2 they (line 6)   6 the variety (line 41)
3 they (line 9)   7 them (line 44)
4 they (line 27)   8 they (line 46)

3 Vocabulary
Find the phrasal verbs in the passage meaning:
1 to begin a journey
2 to die
3 to finish everything so nothing is left

Write your own example sentences for each.

4 Language
Use of verbs in the past
Which tense is used the most in the passage? Why? Underline the instances where a different tense is used. Name the tense and discuss its use (in that particular context) with a partner.

Future in the past
a Look at line 26 in the passage:
Mr Small thought they would make good cooking apples.

The moment of thinking was in the past and Mr Small considered the future from that point in time. We use would + verb to indicate this. We often use this pattern after verbs of thought/speech.

Past ——— Time of thinking *(make good cooking apples)* ——— Now ——► Future
Present

b Complete the following sentences using your imagination about how Granny saw the future.
1 Granny believed the apples ...
2 She hoped they ...
3 She said to her husband they ...
4 She knew her daughters ...
5 She felt ...
6   ... make her famous.

Study Tips

Phrasal verbs The best approach is to learn just a few at a time. Keep a special section in your vocabulary workbook and enter phrasals as you come across them. Enter the phrasal in the infinitive; state if separable or not; give an explanation; an example sentence and a good translation, eg: to come across something or someone; not separable; to find or meet by chance.
I came across my lost pen when I was cleaning the cupboard.

Section C

1 Listen

Listen to this radio interview with Victoria Wood (a British comedienne). As you listen make notes about facts in her life. Use the following headings:

Place   Mother   Father
Brothers/Sisters   Music
Books   Theatre

2 Write

Exam

a Use the information you have collected to complete this text. You will use one or more words in each gap.

b Listen again and check your work.

Learner Skills

- identifying genre of text
- skimming and scanning skills
- interpreting double meaning as humour
- writing as a group activity
- predicting before reading
- finding facts in a text
- inference and reference in a text

Exam Skills

Speaking
B1   interpreting photographs

Reading
B2   true/false statements
Exam

Listening
C1   extracting facts

English in Use
C2   completing text with facts
Exam

Victoria Wood Comedienne

V.W. comes from a family of (1)_____ and two sisters. Now a famous comedienne she (2)_____ and (3)_____ in the North of England near Manchester. She had a close secure family life, living in (4)_____ in the countryside. Both her parents worked: her mother was a teacher and her father, while (5)_____ , was really a semi-professional musician. In his younger days he had (6)_____ but after the war he worked in insurance. His love of music, he passed on to Victoria who played both piano and trumpet though she never imagined she (7)_____ famous, particularly because of her looks. It was not until she (8)_____ at about 15 years old that she began to see the possibility of doing something in the performing arts. Another strong influence on her life was (9)_____ love of books. In fact there were (10)_____ in the house that they were lying around everywhere, taking up a great deal of space. But this led to Victoria, like (11)_____ , becoming an avid reader. Books and music then gave her a sound artistic basis and contributed towards her move into comedy.

THEIR WORK 5

1 Speak

a Discuss this picture. Think of six points to make expressing your opinion.

b In pairs, practise describing the character/s to each other. Make a note of all the adjectives/adjectival phrases you think appropriate.

2 Read

The following text is on the life of Sickert, an influential British artist (1860–1942). A common feature of text organisation is to begin each paragraph with a sentence which introduces the subject/topic of the paragraph.

a Read the title and first paragraph.
Does the first sentence tell us the paragraph is about:

A Winston Churchill
B Churchill's paintings
C Churchill's teacher and their relationship?

b These are the first sentences of the paragraphs 2, 3, 6 and 7. Write beside each the topic you expect the paragraph to be about.

> Sickert was cosmopolitan, witty, highly intelligent, handsome, and immensely popular.

> The trouble was that he would not always serve his own best interests.

> Sickert loved to teach, and was an exceptional teacher, generous, inspiring and insistent upon the highest standards.

> He was prejudiced against women, believing them to be incapable of steady concentration.

Now read the paragraphs and check your answers.

The Master

Walter Sickert's influence is felt in British painting to this day. Maureen Connett traces his life and career

Who taught Winston Churchill to paint? He was a dedicated amateur with an instinctive colour sense who loved to splash about with vivid colour from the start. But he was less enthusiastic about drawing. The steady building-up of a composition had little appeal for him and his teacher had to insist that this was not skimped. His teacher was Walter Sickert. There is a telegram to Sickert which reads:

> *'I am bracing my eyes on Rubens and Rembrandt,*
>
> *Churchill.*

2

Sickert was cosmopolitan, witty, highly intelligent, handsome and immensely popular. Artists, writers, travellers, actors, politicians, students and society hostesses flocked to his studio in Camden Town. Whether he was being entertained by the Churchills at Chartwell or taking a bus ride with a poverty-stricken student, Sickert was always himself — charming, courteous and contradictory. First and foremost, though, he was a painter. A pupil of the great Degas, he never forgot that hard work, a strict routine and the highest standards of discipline and technical skill were what mattered. He was an artist to his fingertips.

3

The trouble was that he would not always serve his own best interests. He gave away numerous paintings to friends or even acquaintances and set absurdly low prices on his pictures. Because he was careless in this way and even perverse, he did not enjoy the popular recognition that he longed for. He is now regarded as our finest painter since Turner but in his own time his enormous talent was more appreciated abroad than at home.

Paragraphs 4 and 5 describe an example of foreign appreciation of Sickert with details of his attitude to buyers.

6

Sickert loved to teach, and was an exceptional teacher, generous, inspiring and insistent upon the highest standards. Yet he was encouraging and gentle with the students. 'At least they are sincere,' he would sigh, as he stood before some beginner's faltering attempt. He held classes in his studio at 8 Fitzroy Street, and his prospectus was designed to weed out the dilettante, though with the greatest care and discretion. He favoured the hard worker, even if little facility was shown. Ability in drawing and painting were not enough; concentration was all-important. He had two main objects in view. One was to encourage students to paint without nature in front of them; the other was to help them to become independent of the schools as soon as possible and find their own level in a wider world.

7

He was prejudiced against women, believing them to be incapable of steady concentration. How much talent he must have discouraged through his blind spot. Here again, his attitude was contradictory, for he steadfastly believed in the undeniably rich talent of Wendela Boreel, a brilliant artist, who excelled in etching and gouache. Sickert would refuse to believe the evidence of his own eyes, maintaining that one or two outstanding women were exceptional. When a woman came under his influence, she would end up either putting her own work a poor second (like Sylvia Gosse, who took over the donkey work of running his school at Rowlandson House), or she would turn out pale copies of his style. This happened with his third wife, Therese Lessore. Before she married him, she used to paint strange little interiors, with a fleeting, fey quality, very much her own. His overpowering personality swamped her and she began instead to echo his subjects. Then she became exclusively interested in him and when he became ill and old, she devoted herself entirely to his welfare.

c Sometimes a short paragraph can function in the same way as an opening sentence. Now read the 8th paragraph and say what the following three paragraphs will be about.

Paragraph 12 is about Sickert's subjects and paragraph 13 describes his approach to painting figures (people).

d These are the first sentences of the paragraphs 14 and 15. Write beside each the topic you expect the paragraph to be about.

> His influence was profound.

> Sickert's influence is still potent today.

Now read the paragraphs and check your answers

15

Sickert's influence is still potent today. His morose and powerful art is akin to that of Dickens, whom he revered. There is the celebration of the variety and poignancy of life, too, and an understanding of its complexities.

e Which of the following is the real last paragraph?

A

You can see examples of Sickert's paintings in the Tate Gallery and many great civic collections. Drawings and etchings occasionally appear at dealers and auction houses. They are now universally prized. He was a profound and masterly artist of whom we can be proud.

B

Dickens wrote about life in all its complexities. Sickert painted life in all its complexities. They complemented each other and should be equally valued and appreciated.

C

Life is full of complexities as Sickert's life was. Perhaps if it had been less so he would have achieved success in his life-time. But perhaps if he had been less complex, the richness and variety of his work would have been lost.

8

Nowhere is Sickert's contradictory quality more evident than in his relationships with women. Although he seemed so independent, he was in fact very much dependent on his three wives, all women of intelligence, refinement and distinction.

14

His influence was profound. Because of his first-hand knowledge of the great French Impressionists, he had a unique authority among a generation of brilliant young painters. They gathered around him in the grey garrets of Fitzroy Street, as eager to learn as he was to teach. Their Saturday afternoon 'At Homes' were convivial occasions. Here, painters and friends met to gossip, consume strong tea and slab cake and occasionally buy and sell paintings. They evolved into the Camden Town Group, a distinct and important circle in the development of British art. Inspired by Sickert, they painted the everyday life around them: informal portraits of working men and women who came in from the streets to model for them; their one bed-sitting rooms, back gardens, London streets and squares, pubs, shops and railway stations.

3 Read

Scan the texts and complete this information grid on Sickert.

> **Walter Sickert**
>
> **Dates:**   **Nationality:**
>
> **Residence:**
>
> **Marital status:**
>
> **Personal strengths:**   **1**
>
>   **2**
>
> **Personal weaknesses: 1**
>
>   **2**
>
> **Personal likes:**
>
> **Character:**

4 Language

Past habits - *would*

a What is the meaning of this sentence in paragraph 3? '*The trouble was he would not always serve his best interests.*' The problem was:

   1 he was not interested in his own problems.

   2 he never used to look after himself.

   3 he quite often did things that were not to his advantage.

b This use of *would* describes a regular past habit or characteristic. Find four other examples of this use of *would*.

c What other word/s also indicate/s past habit? Find the example in paragraph 7.

d Which of the two possibilities are you most likely to use for each of the following:

   1 an informal spoken conversation?

   2 a descriptive monologue like a speech?

   3 a literary novel?

   Can you use both possibilities with the verbs below? Why/why not?

   speak give have (possess) know
   go hope walk complement

e Find five other sentences in the passage which could be written using *would*. Re-write them accordingly.

f Consider your own past habits. Write 10 sentences describing them. Use both patterns.

Section B

Exam

1 Listen

On tape there is an interview with the author of the Sickert article, Maureen Connett.

Read these statements about Maureen. Mark them true or false as you listen.

1 She has very little idea about her readers.
2 She tries to tell a good story.
3 She has to be interested in her subject beforehand.
4 She knew little of Sickert before doing any research.
5 She started her research on Sickert by reading biographies.
6 She understands Sickert fairly well and makes perceptive comments.
7 She only writes about art and artists.
8 She has mixed feelings about Sickert.

Compare your answers. Do you agree?

Exam

2 Listen

Listen again and complete the blanks in the following statements.

The first question the interviewer asks has (1) _____ parts to it. Maureen writes regularly for (2) _____ .

She researches a painter's life in two ways: one by (3) _____ and two (4) _____ the paintings.

Maureen trained originally as (5) _____ .

Sickert was a (6) _____ character. He travelled greatly and spent a lot of time in (7) _____ as well as (8) _____ . (9) _____ dominated his life. Sickert did not realise how much he (10) _____ women.

Maureen writes (11) _____ a month. Maureen thinks of herself as (12) _____ not a critic.

Exam Strategies

Statements on content — Listening. These may be True/False statements. Procedure: read the statements first to focus your listening. As you listen lightly mark T or F. If there is a second listening, check your ideas and mark the answer sheet.

Exam Strategies

Completing numbered gaps — Listening. One or more words may be required. Procedure: read through completely before listening. Then read again noting what information is required. While you listen make notes about the information. The tape is played a second time so while you listen amend your notes. Fill in the gaps checking that grammatical form is correct.

████ Section · C ████

1 Write

a Imagine you have to write a descriptive paragraph on each of these topics:

The Mona Lisa	The Egyptian pyramids
The Himalayas	Sophia Loren
My favourite art form	The leader of my country

For each topic think briefly of the content. Make a few notes, then write a suitable topic sentence to begin each paragraph. Compare and discuss your topic sentences with the class.

b Write a descriptive paragraph of 80–100 words.

Step 1 Choose one of the topics. Add to your notes on content.

Step 2 Organise the points into a logical order following on from the topic sentence.

Step 3 Write the paragraph in rough. Check for errors. Swap with a partner and check theirs for errors.

Step 4 Make any final changes to your own. Write a good copy.

Learner Skills

- studying textual organisation
- predicting topic
- finding specific information in a text
- writing topic sentences
- developing descriptive writing

Exam Skills

A1 *Speaking*
  reacting to and describing a photograph

B1 *Listening*
  true/false statements

B2 *Listening*
Exam completing sentences/summarising text

C *Writing*
Exam descriptive writing

THE PERSON 6

1 Speak

Look at the photo. Say briefly how you would describe this person. What expressions/ adjectives would you use? What sort of life does/did she have? Why do you think that?

2 Listen

Which of the three descriptions fits this person best? Why? Are any of them close to your own?

1 Read

The following texts are all descriptions of people.

a Skim quickly through them and say:
   1 Which describes a black woman/an actor.
   2 Which is written by an observer/a member of their family/an interviewer.
   3 Which takes place in a restaurant/outside/in a house.

b Fill in the blanks in each text with a noun from the list below.

   warmth   seventies
   commitment   gaze   height
   lines   emotions   quality   image
   shoulders   pride   language

Text A
If she'd had her way, my mother would have been an actress. Like the best of them, her presence was irresistible. My father used words to control and keep others at bay. For my mother (1) ...... was a way to reassure and reward. My father demanded loyalty. My mother inspired it in the host of friends whom she cared for and melded into her life. She was a large, buxom woman, with caramel-coloured skin and a serene face that gave little indication of the passion which she imbued every wish, every (2) .... Her hands were large, long-fingered. Serious hands that rendered punishment swiftly and breathlessly, folded sheets and dusted tables in a succession of white folks' homes long after she was mistress of several of her own. Hands that offered unconditional shelter and love. In every picture of her there is freeze-framed a look of sadness rippling across her glance, as though there is still just one more thing she wants to own, to do, to know. She wore perfume, fox fur throws casually slung over her (3) ...... and lamb coats, as though born to wear nothing less. My father confided to me offhandedly once, "When I met your mother I thought she was the most beautiful woman I'd ever seen."

Text B

Three ladies sat there with a man in his (4) .... This man was stiff and elegant, dressed in double-breasted white serge and immaculate shirt and tie. His long, delicate fingers sliced a cold pheasant, almost with daintiness. Yet even in eating he seemed to me unbending, with a ramrod-back, military bearing. His aged face showed "a growing fatigue" but the (5) ...... with which his lips and jaws were set sought desperately to hide the fact, while the eyes twinkled with "the fiery play of fancy."

As the carnival lights of that summer's night in Zurich played with a fire of their own on the features I now recognized, Thomas Mann's face was a theater of implicit, quiet (6) .... He ate and let the ladies do the talking; he was, in my fascinated eyes, a meeting place where solitude gives birth to beauty unfamiliar and perilous, but also to the perverse and the illicit.

Text C

As we chatted and sipped our drinks by the fire in her sitting-room, I gained some impression of the presence Dame Flora Robson must have carried with her on stage. She has never been conventionally beautiful, but this very fact has given her face an enduring (7) ...... that even now, in her early eighties, remains. In actual fact, nothing could be more beautiful than the very strength of her features: the wide, full curve of her lips and the large, deep-blue eyes that seem to drink in everything around her. And though she has lost two inches off her original (8) ...... of five foot nine, she still stands with the erectness and moves with all the graceful assurance of the trained performer. Like her handclasp, everything about her is firm and direct, though gentle.

In this atmosphere of relaxed (9) ...... it seemed natural to talk first about her family, which was for Flora the emotional foundation on which her career rested. She was the sixth of seven children, five girls and two boys, born to Eliza McKenzie, a sea-captain's daughter who had married David Robson, her father's second engineer. Both of them had moved from their native Scotland to South Shields, where David Robson worked as a marine surveyor in a Tyneside shipbuilding firm. This is where, on 28 March 1902, Flora Robson was born. Since she was born on a Good Friday, her godmother said that all her sins would be forgiven.

Text D

The most vivid (10) ...... I have of Naomi Mitchison comes from watching her walking around the large and multifarious garden at Carradale in Scotland, her home base for nearly fifty years. She was naming the plants for me. There were an incredible variety of rhododendrons. Down at the bottom of the garden, over a wind-blown field, was the sea.

Having talked to Naomi Mitchison about her life, Carradale seemed to me at once a haven and a stepping-off point. The woman by my side was thoroughly rooted here. Yet, I felt, this very rootedness gave her the freedom to set out on innumerable journeys. I could visualise her walking out of her front door and down to the sea, stepping casually into a small waiting boat and disappearing over the water.

Everything about Naomi Mitchison bespeaks a kind of fearlessness. Her movements are decisive and energetic. Her face, whose strong features and uncompromising expressions were once captured in the drawings of Wyndham Lewis, has lost none of its intensity. It has, naturally enough, gained a great many (11) ......, which, when she reflects on some question you have asked her, almost swallow up the rest of the face in a movement of concentration, a sort of indrawing out of which her eyes will suddenly emerge to fix yours with their piercing blue (12) .... Those eyes are what I see when I think of her frank and witty responses to my often rather intimate questions about her life.

c Read Text A and answer these questions.
What did the mother want to do?
What work did she do?
What did she own in her life?
Was she a loving mother?
How did she dress?
Was she weak or strong?
What might her friends have thought of her?
What does her daughter think of her?

Read Text B and answer these questions.
Who was the character with?
How would you describe his dress?
What contradiction is noted by the writer?
What was he trying to hide?
Did the author know who the man was?
What was the writer's feeling?

Read Text C and answer these questions.
  Was Dame Flora Robson a beautiful
    woman?
  What was the most outstanding feature in
    her face?
  How was her family important to her?
  What nationality were her parents?
  Where did her father first work?
  Who was his boss?
  How did she treat her interviewer?
  How would you describe this woman?

Read Text D and answer these questions.
  What did Naomi Mitchison do while they
    were walking around the garden?
  How important was Carradale for her?
  What did it give her?
  What had Wyndham Lewis done to her?
  What was (probably) his job?
  How old roughly was Naomi at the time of
    the interview?
  What facial feature clearly impressed the
    interviewer?
  How did Naomi react to the interviewer's
    questions?

d Identify sections of the texts where we are:
  • given a description of character.
  • given physical description.
  • given factual information about the person's life.
  • given a combination of information.

2 Language

Comparison

a Find examples in texts A and C where comparison is used to enhance the description. State who/what is compared in each case.

b *Like* + noun phrase may begin, or may finish, a sentence. Rewrite the two examples in the text in the alternative way. Write five of your own examples describing people using *like* in both positions.

c *As though* + verb phrase is used to introduce a comparison whether 'real' or 'unreal'.

Both the examples in Text A are 'unreal'. Say why. What words have been elided in the second example?

Yet in initial position

Scan the texts and find the two examples of sentences beginning with *yet*. What is the meaning of *yet* in each case: 1 in addition   2 but   3 for?

Does the author use *yet* to indicate:
1 surprise   2 anger   3 dislike at the following
                                  information?

Having + past participle in initial position

a Look at this sentence in Text D.
  Having talked to Naomi ... Carradale seemed to me ...

We use *Having* + past participle at the beginning of a sentence when we mean 'as a result of'. The second clause of the sentence is the result/consequence of the earlier action.

Study Tips

Ellipsis   This is a common feature of many languages. It is not always necessary to say/write every grammatical word if such words are understood from the context. For example: *I ran into the room and picked up the child*. The second *I* before *picked up* is elided but it would not be wrong to include it. It is advisable to make a note of particular forms which can be elided. But be careful: for each grammatical pattern different rules apply. It is also useful to identify where ellipsis occurs and analyse what words have been elided.

We could rewrite the sentence using *because*.

Because I had talked to Naomi... Carradale seemed to me ...

It is also possible to negate or modify the phrase using *not* or adverbs of frequency before the having.

Never/ Not having talked to him, I could not know the answer.
Because I had never talked to him, I could not know the answer.

b Complete these sentences using *having* + an appropriate verb then rewrite them using *because*.
   1 ... the extract, I'd like to read the book.
   2 ... how she looked at 90, it was no surprise to learn she was a famous beauty in her youth.
   3 ... there before, I was totally lost.
   4 ... her, he considered his duty complete.
   5 ... the play, I cannot comment.
   6 Seldom ... his home town, he was totally lost in Paris.

Compound words
There are several examples of compound adjectives and nouns in the texts. Compound nouns are often formed with two singular nouns.

a Look through the texts and make two lists: compound adjectives and compound nouns.

b For each adjective think of other nouns you could describe with each, for example:
a fiery-red sunset/car/dress

For each noun write an equivalent noun phrase, for example:
a car door = a door of a car.

c Make the compound noun for each of these phrases:
a woman with a career.
an actor specialised in theatre.
a clown who works in a circus.
an article in a newspaper.
an advert shown on television.
a computer for personal use.
a house built of red brick.
a car made as a toy.

3 Vocabulary
Look back at Texts A–D and make two lists of the adjectives used to describe:
   1 personality/behaviour.
   2 physical features.

Compare your lists and discuss the meaning of these words. Give examples of people you know to whom these adjectives could be applied.

1 Speak

Work on your own and prepare an oral description of somebody you know. Think of their character, life, work and physical features. Make notes, do not write sentences. Give your talk (about 1 minute), to the class.

Listen to the others' talks. Make a note of one grammar or vocabulary question to ask at the end of each talk. After the talk, ask your question.

Study Tips

Long speaking turns It is important to develop your ability to speak for some time — a long speaking turn. Think what you want to say, make notes of the content, and organise them in an effective order. You must not write sentences in your preparation because this will result in written language being read aloud instead of spoken language. This is a very important distinction.

The ability to speak for some time on your own will develop your confidence in speaking English and is also important for the Speaking paper of the examination.

1 Listen

Exam

Who is being described? There are five descriptions on tape. Put them in the order in which you hear them by writing a number from 1 to 5 in each box.

an old man ☐   a baby ☐   a lover ☐
a teacher ☐   a hero ☐   heroine ☐   a soldier ☐

Listen again. Which are poetic and which are factual?

Learner Skills

- developing confidence speaking
- doing detailed comprehension of text
- analysing the purpose of text
- understanding ellipsis
- organising vocabulary by category

2 Write

Exam

Use some of the information given in this unit and write a description (about 100 words) of one of the characters in D1. The character you choose may be imaginary or real.

Step 1   Make notes about what you want to include. Make a list of vocabulary. Consider all aspects — character, physical features, work, lifestyle, etc.

Step 2   Organise your notes into sections and decide on a logical order. The sections may vary in length. Consider the order carefully. The most important sections should be central.

Step 3   Think of an introductory first sentence (topic sentence) and a concluding last sentence (summarising the person).

Step 4   Write a draft version, following your notes.

Step 5   Swap your draft with a partner. Read your partner's and then, work together to correct and improve each others' paragraphs.

Step 6   Write the final copy. Stick the descriptions on the wall. Discuss the paragraphs with the class.

Exam Skills

A1   *Speaking*
        describing someone in a photo

A2   *Listening*
        matching speaker

B1b *English in Use*
        developing gap filling skill

C   *Speaking*
        developing long turn speaking

D1   *Listening*
Exam   matching topic and tone

D2   *Writing*
Exam   describing people

EXAM SECTION

Female victory against male odds

BRIGHT SPARK

Breakthroughs and those behind them. This week: **Elizabeth Garrett Anderson** (1836–1917).

The first woman in Britain to undergo medical training and qualify as a doctor was Elizabeth Garrett Anderson. In 1859 she heard the American physician Dr Elizabeth Blackwell lecture and decided to follow her example.

This meant breaking the male monopoly of the British medical profession. Garrett Anderson began by becoming a nurse at Middlesex Hospital in London.

She was admitted to lectures and topped the examinations, but jealous male students resented her and after a year's classes she was barred. Not to be put off, she approached many other medical schools, but in vain. Eventually, the Society of Apothecaries agreed to examine her. Garret Anderson tried to enrol at several universities, but they all rejected her. However, the Society of Apothecaries accepted courses taught by private tuition and in 1865 she passed their examination.

Garrett Anderson started in private practice in London but was not too busy to organise an early campaign for womens' votes. In 1866 she opened the St Mary's dispensary for Women and Children. She also sat for a degree in France, becoming Paris University's first woman MD in 1870.

That October she stood and won election to the London School Board running primary schools. Her marriage in 1871 did not stop her joining the committee building Girton College for women a Cambridge, or opening the New Hospital for Women in London in 1872. In 1874 Garrett Anderson became the first woman member of the British Medical Association and she started lecturing at the new London School of Medicine for Women, where she was appointed Dean in 1883.

Throughout the 1880s she raised money for a bigger Hospital for Women, completed in 1889 and later renamed after her. In 1898 she oversaw construction of a larger School of Medicine which, in 1902, joined London University.

Elizabeth Garrett Anderson retired that year but after her husband died in 1907, she achieved a final British first, succeeding him as Mayor of Aldeburgh, Suffolk.

Read this newspaper article. Below there are a number of questions or unfinished statements about the text. You must choose the answer which you think fits best.

1 Dr Blackwell
   a lectured to E. Garrett at university.
   b inspired E. Garrett to enter medicine.
   c motivated E. Garrett to start lecturing.
   d was an example teacher to E. Garrett.

2 E. Garrett was prohibited from continuing her studies because
   a of the attitude of her fellow students.
   b she did not do well in examinations.
   c she distracted her male colleagues.
   d of her attitude to her colleagues.

3 She eventually studied for her medical degree
   a at a different university.
   b with personal tutors.
   c at a private college.
   d at the Society of Apothecaries.

4 As a woman she was particularly interested in
   a political movements.
   b being recognised.
   c equal rights for women.
   d children.

5 Apart from medicine she also was involved in
   a women's health, teaching children, and building hospitals.
   b building hospitals, education and the use of drugs.
   c teaching children, politics and voting.
   d politics, education, teaching women, and fund raising.

6 You could describe her life as being
   a easy and satisfying.
   b studious and intellectual.
   c extremely active and happy.
   d challenging and full of achievement.

LISTENING Section D

You will hear five commentaries on various people's lives.

Task One lists the nationality of the people. Put them in the order in which you hear them by writing a number from 1 to 5 in each box. Three boxes will remain empty.

Canadian ☐   Scottish ☐

Nigerian ☐   New Zealander ☐

American ☐   Australian ☐

Welsh ☐   English ☐

Task Two lists the work that made these people famous. Put the commentaries in the order in which you hear them by writing numbers 1 to 5 in the appropriate boxes. Three boxes will remain empty.

author ☐   politician ☐

poet ☐   singer ☐

doctor ☐   artist ☐

architect ☐   detective ☐

Exam Strategies

Match ranking — Listening. One or two tasks on a series of extracts. You have to identify something like topic, speaker, tone, function. You will only have to write numbers/letters in the boxes. Procedure: read the instructions and the lists carefully. Not all the alternatives will be used, so for 5 extracts the list may be 8. As you listen, fill in the numbers. Use a pencil at first. Fill in the answers in ink after you finish listening. It is very important to understand exactly what is being asked for before listening.

ENGLISH IN USE   Section B

In most lines of the following text there is one word missing. Read the text, mark with a / where the word should go and then write the word in the space provided at the end of the line. Some lines are correct. Indicate these lines with a tick against the line number. The first two lines have been done as examples.

Margaret Atwood

1	was born in Ottawa in 1939. She spent much of/early life in the	**her** 1
2	Northern Ontario and Quebec bush country and started writing at the age	✓ 2
3	of five. A graduate from the University of Toronto, where she won a	_____ 3
4	Woodrow Wilson Fellowship, with Masters degree from Radcliffe College,	_____ 4
5	she has travelled extensively and held a wide of jobs.	_____ 5
6	M. Atwood is Canada's most eminent novelist, poet and critic. Her first	_____ 6
7	volume poetry, *The Circle Game* (1966), won the governor-General's Award.	_____ 7
8	Since she has published nine volumes of poetry and a study of Canadian	_____ 8
9	Literature, *Survival*. Her first novel *The Edible Woman* published	_____ 9
10	in 1969, followed *Surfacing*, *Lady Oracle*, *Life Before Man*, *Bodily Harm*,	_____ 10
11	*The Handmaid's Tale*, shortlisted for the Booker Prize and winner of	_____ 11
12	the Governor-General's Award, and *Cat's Eye*, also shortlisted the	_____ 12
13	Booker Prize. She has also two collections of short stories, *Dancing*	_____ 13
14	*Girls* and *Bluebeard's Egg*. M. Atwood lives in Toronto the writer	_____ 14
15	Graeme Gibson and their daughter.	_____ 15

Exam Strategies

Proof-reading — English in Use.   Procedure: skim read the whole text. Note any illogicalities. Go back to the beginning and read the first sentence. Check the grammatical form, look for phrases which do not make sense, and try to identify where/what/if something is missing line by line. Read the next sentence. What connection is there with the preceding one? Is a linking word required? Now check the sentence itself. Continue through the text. Check your answers. Write them on the sheet.

WRITING Section B

Your answer should follow the instructions given. Write approximately 250 words.

You are to enter an English Language Competition in your country. As part of your entry you must write a descriptive essay on somebody's life. The person may be alive or dead, famous or unknown. The essay should describe this person in an interesting fashion. It could include giving a view of their character, looks, background, achievements, life-style, thoughts or influence.

ROLES

7

1 Listen

a You will hear five words. Write the first two words you think of when you hear each of the five words

b Listen again. Write down the original words. What do you feel about each of them? Are they negative, positive or neutral?

c Compare your work with a partner. Do you agree about the feel of each word? Look back at the words you wrote in **a**. Do you have any similar associated words?

d Work together and see how many related words you can form from each of the original five. Identify the part of speech. For example: friend (noun), friendly (adjective), friendship (noun). Write an example sentence using each word.

Study Tips

Connotation   Words often have a 'hidden' meaning. In many cases, a particular word is understood in a particular way. This may be negative or positive eg: *slim* is positive but *skinny* is negative implying criticism. Sometimes people have their own feelings about certain words because of their personal experience of life.

1 Language

a Look at the first photo. Discuss the possible relationship between the people. Make a list of different ways to express possibility.

b Check your list. You should have used patterns beginning with:
Maybe...   It looks as if...   It's possible...

What is a synonym for *maybe/it looks/if*?

2 Discuss

a Study both photographs and consider the relationship between the people, the mood and the quality of the relationship.

b Discuss your ideas. Explain your opinions. Do you agree? Think of different interpretations. Which interpretation do you prefer? Have the photographers been successful in conveying the feelings and the moods?

c Report your ideas and opinions to the class.

3 Listen

a Listen to the five people each describing a particular relationship. Match the speaker to the relationship. Match the adjective in the list which best describes each relationship.

b Think of alternative adjectives to describe these relationships.

☐ neighbours   ☐ difficult

☐ cousins   ☐ cool

☐ brothers   ☐ loving

☐ work colleagues   ☐ angry

☐ child/parent   ☐ close

4 Language

Expressing annoyance

Two of the speakers on the tape express annoyance with another person's particular habits. Listen to these expressions in isolation and write down the exact words. Mark which word is stressed each time. Which pattern is the past of another? Put the other three patterns into the past.

Listen again and practise saying each phrase.

5 Speak

Think of an annoying habit of: a member of your family, pop stars, politicians, yourself when you were a child, your teacher. Tell each other about these habits, using the different patterns from the tape.

Section C

1 Read

Study these messages.

1 Who wrote each message and to whom?
2 Where could you see each note?
3 What is the situation?
4 What is the purpose of the message?

Back in ten minutes.

Dear Jane, Thank you for the book. It is lovely. We had a good Christmas I hope you did. Love Alison.

Darling-
When you get in ... pop round the shops and get some milk and eggs. Sorry - I'm working late ...
Put dinner on.
        Love you.

2 Write

Messages like the above are written in a casual style. You do not need to write in complete sentences, and vocabulary is colloquial.
Divide into A's and B's.

A's write the following messages:
1 A parent telling a teenage child to phone a friend.
2 An office worker asking a colleague to attend a meeting.

B's write these messages:
3 An adult asking a teenager to babysit.
4 A note to a neighbour asking them not to park in front of your house.

Andy - Could you type this for me please? I've got an urgent meeting. Thanks a lot.

The postman couldn't get an answer so he left a parcel with me. Just ring - I'll be in all evening.

Section D

1 Discuss
How do you react to this photo?

2 Read
a Skim the text and see if this description matches your own ideas of stereotypical husband/wife roles.

The 'Doll's House' and the hen-pecked husband...

Robin Well, there are more kinds of middle-range marriages than there are types of trees, so we'll just have to select one or two as examples. A very common one is a type we call a 'Doll's House' marriage, after the play by Ibsen. Here the couple have taken on very stereotyped male and female roles. He appears the big, strong man, very grown up and parental; and she's the poor, helpless little woman, very childish and dependent.

5 **John** Remind me about the story. The husband gets ill and the wife saves his life by taking him abroad ...

Robin And she has to make sacrifices to get the money for the trip. But the point of the story is that she has to keep those sacrifices hidden from her husband because she believes it would destroy him — that is, it would dent his male pride too hopelessly — if he ever discovered how much he owes to her. In other words, if he sees how dependent he really is on her.

10 **John** So a 'Doll's House' marriage is one where it's obvious that the wife is emotionally dependent on the husband; but he's dependent on her too, but doesn't know it. And they both behave as though he isn't.

Robin Right. He has been taught that males must be strong and independent. They never cry, they never need looking after. But he's been forced to grow up too quickly. Therefore he's had to suppress, rather than *grow out of*, childish needs to be looked after. So there's a hidden, unsatisfied baby in him.

Exam **b** Read these statements about the text carefully. Are they true or false?

1 There are many other types of marital relationships.
2 The husband (in the play) would have died but for his wife.
3 The wife (in the play) had no trouble getting the money.
4 The husband knew all about his wife's sacrifices.
5 He became financially dependent on his wife.
6 He saw strength in the equality of men and women.
7 He had never cried as a baby.
8 He knowingly wanted his wife to take care of him.

c 'The couple' in line 3 is our first introduction to the two characters (husband and wife). From then on they are referred to as 'he' and 'she'. Using two different colours, ring each of the subsequent references to both these characters. What do the following words refer to?

it (line 7) it (line 7) it (line 10) it (line 11)

Study Tips

Prediction We seldom read anything without having some idea of the content beforehand. This is because the title/headline/caption/photograph/topic, etc, subconsciously activates all we know and we form expectations. Certain activities are therefore included before listening and reading texts in order to consciously (and subconsciously) activate your own knowledge, opinions and expectations as a strategy towards aiding your comprehension.

3 Vocabulary

a Find the following phrases in the text. What is the meaning of each in this context?

1 to take on a role
   A to wear a costume
   B to behave in a certain way
   C to act

2 to make sacrifices
   A to kill animals
   B to give 'things' to the church
   C to deprive oneself of something

3 to dent someone's pride
   A to increase someone's pride
   B to damage someone's pride
   C to benefit someone's pride

4 to suppress
   A to squash
   B to supplement
   C to surrender

b Make lists of all the words/phrases in the text which you think are often related to men and to women. Explain your choice of words. Discuss whether you accept this use of words as right or wrong.

4 Language

Adverbial clauses with *so*

a Underline the three clauses introduced by *so*. In the first example, does *so* introduce:
   1 the purpose of preceding action/behaviour?
   2 the conclusion to/result of preceding information?
   Which of the above does *so* introduce in the other examples?

b Accept that what they are saying in the passage is true and write five sentences expressing your own conclusions using *so*.
   Note: *so* plus result clause usually occurs in initial position except with the conjunction and.

Tenses for relating a plot

a Find the section in the text where the plot of the play is described. What tense is used? Why do you think that is?

b Think of a play (or a novel/film) which you know and prepare a short talk outlining the plot. Remember only make notes in your preparation. Do not write sentences. Begin by stating what the central theme is and then briefly introduce the characters and say what happens. Use the Simple Present.

Learner Skills

- associating words
- work on connotation
- understanding relationships/mood
- work on stress to show annoyance
- interpreting purpose and context of text
- informal writing
- predicting text content
- work on reference
- work on vocabulary in context
- giving short talk

Exam Skills

B1/2 *Speaking*
developing skill of interpreting photos

B3
Exam *Listening*
matching speaker, relationships, tone

D2b
Exam *Reading*
true/false statements

D3 *English in Use*
meaning of vocabulary in text for multiple choice

FRIENDS AND COLLEAGUES

8

1 Vocabulary

a This is an old saying. What is your own reaction to it? In groups think of reasons why it is a dog. Would you replace dog with any other animal?

As this is an old saying we can understand man to mean all human beings. However, consider it does mean only men. Would you change your opinion? What if you substituted women or children?

b Think of other sayings/idioms using the word *dog*, in English and in your own language. Prepare examples which demonstrate the meanings.

"*A dog is a man's best friend*,,

2 Language
Defining relative clauses

a Write a definition of 'a best friend'. Compare the patterns you have used with a partner.

What pattern is used in this example?
Best friends are people (who/that) you can usually ring up at the most impossible hours...

With these clauses we can sometimes omit certain words, or use alternative pronouns.

b Combine each pair of sentences to make one sentence.
 1 An enemy is someone. An enemy wants to harm you.
 2 Some people are too friendly at first. I don't trust some people.
 3 You should value friendship. Friendship is something valuable.
 4 You cannot deny bonds. Shared experience creates bonds.
 5 The letter is lying on my desk. The letter is from my closest friend.

c In more traditional English a combination of preposition and pronoun are used, for example:
She knows someone with whom she can discuss the matter.

Now, we are more likely to say:
She knows someone (who) she can discuss the matter with.

Rewrite the following using the second pattern.
1 He was invited by someone with whom he works.
2 I saw the boy to whom the prize was given.
3 She left the house in which she had been so happy.
4 They found someone to whom they could talk.
5 She gave up the job to which she had dedicated her life.

Combine the information into one sentence.
6 I've got a colleague. I cannot work with that colleague.
7 You don't have to explain things to a best friend. A best friend is a person.
8 You can confide in some friends. Friends are invaluable.
9 You can never relax with some people. There are people.
10 You could never apply yourself to some jobs. There are jobs.

3 Listen

Exam

Read through the following list of 'qualities' in best friends. Listen and mark which speaker mentions which qualities. (In some cases there is more than one speaker). Write the initial/s of the speaker beside each statement. The speakers are in this order: Bruce, Stephanie, Rita, Alison and Jeremy.

Exam Strategies

Multiple match — Listening. (See also Reading multiple match page 51) A matching exercise when options can be used more than once. Procedure: read the options very carefully. Make sure you understand what to do. As you listen to each speaker try to match them with the relevant option. Remember a speaker may give you more than one piece of information.

Qualities in best friends

A best friend lasts for years and years. _____

A best friend is someone who does things for you. _____

Best friends talk about close personal issues and secrets. _____

Best friends like being and doing things together. _____

Best friends change as you change. _____

Best friends understand each other easily. _____

A best friend is someone who can contact you anytime. _____

4 Speak

What do you think about best friends? Which of the above qualities do you agree with? Add two 'qualities'.
Work with a partner and look at your combined list of 'qualities'. Select the five you agree are the most important. Then arrange them in a scale of 1 to 5, with 1 being the most important quality.

5 Pronunciation

a When we speak we use 'chunks' each usually containing one piece of information. Read the transcript while you listen to Bruce again. Mark the start and finish of each chunk with a /. An example is given.

b Now listen again and underline the word or words which are most heavily stressed in each chunk. What can you say about these words?

Best friends are friends that you have who you stick by most of your life / ... I've got a few best friends who I have now and some who were best friends at times before but I've still got a strong relationship with.... Yeah, they do lots of things for you, normally they're close to you and you always share your deepest feelings and secrets with them.

6 Write

a Paragraph A represents a written report of what Stephanie said on tape. Read through then listen again. Ask the teacher any questions you may have. Discuss the differences between the spoken and written versions. Read the transcript on page 173.

Exam **b** Listen again to Jeremy.
Complete paragraph B by adding one or two words in each blank. The first one has been done for you. Check the transcript on page 173.

Exam Strategies

Rewriting in a different register — English in Use. You are given information in a particular style and you have to add to the outline/notes given to re-present the information in a different style/register. For example, from informal to formal, or spoken to written. Procedure: skim the information. Skim read the outline. Make sure you understand the difference. Consider the first sentence (one or more blanks included) and think what information is wanted. Find the information. Fill in the blanks paying particular attention to: the grammar, the choice of lexis, the appropriacy. Work step by step through the outline.

A

Best friends are very important in most people's lives. In the situation where you do not have a best friend and you cannot talk to a brother or sister, then, it is as if something were missing in your life. Everybody needs to talk to somebody about, say, problems they have at home or about the opposite sex. Basically people who do not have a best friend are very lonely.

B

Best friends according to Jeremy.

Best friends are **people** whom you, if you have a problem, can usually telephone at (1)_____ hours.

I (2) _____ have one or two very good friends.

(3) _____ we do not see each other regularly, when we do meet we (4) _____ to enter into deep, serious conversation without the (5) _____ following (6) _____ conventions first. We are able to get to the (7) _____ of the matter and we seem to be able to assimilate the changes in our lives (8) _____ .

1 Read

a Read the title and caption of the text. What is the theme of the article? Is the title written or spoken language? What piece of language gives you a clue? Who do you think writes/says it to whom?

Exam **b** Now read quickly through these unfinished statements and alternatives. Select the best alternatives after reading the text.

1 The writer's sister
   A could not stand Richard.
   B thought Richard could be attractive.
   C thought Richard had a charming eccentric personality.
   D asked questions about Richard.

2 Many people only have friends who
   A keep themselves away from the rest of the world.
   B like each other.
   C are exactly like themselves.
   D are academics.

3 What did the writer's Irish friend teach her?
   A That drunken husbands are a problem.
   B To see the funny side in everything.
   C Not to get married.
   D To always consider oneself as important.

4 The writer's friend, the secretary,
   A always brings office work home.
   B has trouble sleeping.
   C thinks family life is almost as important as work.
   D does not allow work problems to interfere with home/social life.

5 According to the writer what kind of friends are best?
   A Ones who support you in everything you do.
   B Ones who help you.
   C Ones who show you how to keep perspective on life.
   D Ones who bring variety to your life.

2 Speak

Look at the text and make a list of the four phrases which describe the types of friends she has. Using these patterns make your own list of the types of friends you have. Give an identifying feature for each.

Exchange your list with a partner and discuss all the types of friends, their qualities, their value.

What on earth do you see in those friends?

Being surrounded by friends who are different helps give you new insight into yourself

By Linda Franklin.

"Whatever do you see in him?" my sister once asked, with undisguised horror, about Richard. I looked at him through her eyes and saw an anti-social, foul-mouthed recluse with a nervous twitch, dirty fingernails and scruffy hair wearing a stained duffel coat and bagged corduroy trousers. But through my eyes he's an endearing eccentric, a sharp intellectual and wit who shares with me both his one-off insights into people and the vulnerable side of his personality. He's been one of my best friends for 14 years now. And not one of my other friends likes him. We've all seen people who like to be surrounded by clones of themselves: academics, for instance, who know of nothing outside their own world; and debs, say, who insulate themselves from the rest of the world by always sticking together. But I couldn't imagine anything more boring than having friends who all seem the same — and just like me. What fun is there in seeing people again and again who share all your interests, never disagree with you and are all in the same position in life?

I've learned a lot by making friends from different walks of life: there was the Irish barmaid I used to work with who had an unfaithful husband and two awful children, and who drank too much and was always broke but who taught me that, no matter what happened, none of it was that important and you could find something to laugh at in every situation. Then there's my friend who works as a secretary and believes a home and social life count just as much as work, if not more, and refuses ever to lose a moment's sleep over office problems. And then there's the friend who works with sexually abused children and could really tell you what matters in this world. Friends like these can go a long way to putting some balance in your life, as their example helps you to assess your own priorities.

3 Vocabulary

a Find the following idioms and phrasal verbs in the text.
to look through someone's eyes
to stick together
walks of life
to be broke
to see something in someone

b Use one of the above in an appropriate form to complete these sentences.
1 There was such a variety of people there; they came from all different ...
2 When things get difficult friends have got ...
3 James had to pay for his brother you know; Paul ... .
4 I couldn't stand her boss but ... he could do no wrong.
5 Pamela, I can't ... . She's boring, unfriendly and snobby.

c Write your own examples of each.

Section   C

1 Listen

a Note three characteristics of a typical employee/boss relationship. Compile a class list of characteristics you all agree about.

b On tape there are extracts from three separate conversations on this topic. For each say:

1 what the problem is in the employee/boss relationship.
2 what the relationship is between the speakers.
3 if the listener is sympathetic or not.

2 Speak

Make a list of the characteristics of:
a a good boss/employee relationship.
b a good teacher/student relationship.

Exchange lists and explain/justify your choice of items.

Learner Skills

- understanding idiomatic meaning
- interpreting speaker's meaning
- assessing and negotiating
- work on rhythm, nuclear stress and information chunks
- identifying features of written versus spoken register
- explaining and justifying oneself

Exam Skills

A3 Exam	*Listening* multiple match	
A4	*Speaking* working out an agreement	
A6b Exam	*English in Use* writing in different registers	
B1b Exam	*Reading* multiple choice	
C1	*Listening* interpreting context and tone	
C2	*Speaking* exchanging information	

TEENAGERS

9

1 Vocabulary

a Look at this newspaper headline. What do you think the article will be about? What word/s could replace *strangely*? What does the use of this word imply?

Teenagers
strangely happy
with their lot

b Does their lot mean their belongings, their collection (for example: stamps), or their situation in life?

c As a class think of all the possible adjectives used to describe teenagers. Divide these into negative, positive and neutral. Compare your categorisation with others.

2 Read

a As you read, list the ways in which teenagers are happy. Fill in the blanks with one word selected from the list below.
too   enough   such   about   only

b Read the article and work out what questions were asked in the survey. Write them out in the style of a questionnaire (see page 47). Decide what other questions would be of value to a survey of this type. Add them. Keep this piece of work. You will use it later.

Young People today are strangely content. Unlike many generations before them, they don't seem to have many arguments with the way their lives are run.

The British teenagers' lot is a happy one, and parents are not the ogres we all love to think they are, according to the second exclusive Indy survey on the mood of our readership.

Indeed, home is (1) _____ a sweet place that 79 per cent of you do not want to leave it before the age of 18. One person does not want to leave at all. Only three per cent say the atmosphere in their homes is unfriendly.

The Indy asked 500 12–15-year-olds how happy they were at home, and their parents came up smelling of roses. Ninety-two per cent of Indy teenagers are happy with the amount their parents listen to them. Seventy-two per cent feel they have (2) _____ status at home.

More than half of parents share interests with their kids, ranging from drag racing and physics, to art and flower arranging.

Rarely are parents considered to be (3) _____ tough: 74 per cent of our teenagers say discipline at home is (4) _____ right, and 13 per cent complain their parents aren't tough enough.

Parents are held in such high regard that 66 per cent of our teenagers would consider looking after them when they grow too old to live by themselves.

But while parents might take comfort from our findings, not everyone will be happy at what the survey reveals.

Teachers might not like to know that parents supervise homework in (5) _____ 21 per cent of cases.

Feminists should be displeased to learn that teenagers generally consider their fathers to be boss of the house. In only 26 per cent of homes was power shared equally between both parents.

Authoritarians will be angry to discover that 47 per cent of our teenagers are not expected home until 10pm or later.

3 Language

Determiners - *such*

a Which of the following words in the list below can be qualified with *such* and which with *such a*?

good sense   bad   big heart   high esteem   very happy
friendly mother   self-centred   wonderful friends
late at night   difficult relationship   strange man

b Work out the rules for choosing *such* or *such a*.

c What intensifiers can you use before each?

Inversion after adverbs of frequency

The word order of subject and verb changes when we begin a sentence with a negative adverb of frequency or adverbial phrase.

a Make a list of adverbs of frequency. Separate out those with a negative meaning/connotation.

b Find the two examples of inversion in the text. Rewrite the sentences using a different order which does not require inversion.

c Complete the following sentences.

1 Seldom _____ her so happy.
2 _____ has any understanding of the child.
3 Never _____ such an opportunity again.
4 So _____ seen that people become suspicious.
5 _____ ever _____ the results of these surveys.
6 _____ 3 per cent of the cases _____ .

d Write another five examples about people using different adverbs.

enough as a qualifier

Look at the examples in the text. What rule about word order applies when *enough* qualifies a noun, an adjective, an adverb?

4 Vocabulary

a Find the word/phrases which mean:
results   to vary between   strict
on the authority of   used only by us

b Underline the phrases in A in the passage.

Choose the best substitute phrase for each from B.

A	B
came up smelling of roses	*are respected greatly*
is about right	*is not right nor wrong*
are held in such high regard	*held up as examples*
take comfort from	*feel happier because of*
	never smell bad
	were praised
	is more or less as it should be
	understand

5 Listen

Some teenagers were interviewed using The Indy survey questionnaire.

Listen to the interview and see if the questions you identified in A2b are the same. Make a note of any differences.

Section B

1 Discuss

Work with a partner. A look at photo 2 on page 169. B look at photo 5 on page 171. Without looking at each other's photos find out if there is anything in common and if there are any differences.

2 Discuss

Think about your neighbours at home. Choose either a particular person or something that happened with a neighbour. Make a few notes describing the person or the event.

Exchange your descriptions in small groups. Have any of you had similar neighbours or experiences? Can you agree on 'the ideal neighbour'? Agree on some characteristics.

Exam Strategies

Information gap — Speaking.
(Phase B) You and your partner will have similar photographs. Your task is to find out the relationship between the photos, identify similarities, differences, any relationship between them. Procedure: study your photo. Begin describing. Your partner must listen carefully and can ask questions for more detail when you finish. Your partner has to say what the relationship is or what the difference are or what the similarities are between the photographs. Do you agree? Discuss further until you are both satisfied.

3 Write

Below you will find the questions asked in a survey into Neighbourliness and the statistical results. Write an article for the local newspaper reporting and commenting briefly on the survey.

Step 1 List all the points you wish to make, then decide on the best order to present them.

Step 2 Outline an introductory and concluding paragraph (these need not be too long).

Step 3 Write a draft version of each paragraph. Proof-read checking the grammar, the spelling and the appropriacy of the vocabulary.

Step 4 Give your article a headline. Write a final version 90 to 120 words long.

Questionnaire

1 How many people do you know the names of in your street?
  a none   b 1–5   c 5–10   d over 10
2 How many neighbours do you consider friends?
  a none   b 1–5   c 5–10   d over 10
3 How many do you consider acquaintances — you say good morning, ask after their family, chat about the weather?
  a none   b 1–5   c 5–10   d over 10
4 How many could you call for help in an emergency?
  a none   b 1–5   c 5–10   d over 10
5 Do any of your neighbours have a spare key to your house?
  a yes   b no   c don't know/understand
6 Do you have a spare key to any of your neighbours' houses?
  a yes   b no   c don't know/understand
7 Would you leave a spare key with a neighbour if you went away for a month?
  a yes   b no   c don't know/understand
8 Would you tell any of your neighbours that you are going away before a holiday?
  a yes   b no   c don't know/understand
9 Have you had any trouble/disagreements with neighbours?
  a yes   b no   c don't know/understand
10 You are having a party, would you invite any of your neighbours?
  a yes   b no   c don't know/understand

Results

	a	b	c	d
1	40	44	13	3
2	68	28	3	1
3	23	45	21	11
4	12	68	13	7
5	43	51	6	
6	38	54	8	
7	63	32	5	
8	83	11	6	
9	35	57	8	
10	43	41	16	

EXAM SECTION

ENGLISH IN USE   Section B

In most lines of the following text there is one unnecessary word. It is either grammatically incorrect or does not fit in with the sense of the text.

Read the text (an excerpt from a magazine article), put a line through each unnecessary word and then write the word in the space provided at the end of the line. Some lines are correct. Indicate these lines with a tick (✓) against the line number. The first two lines have been done as examples.

Exam Strategies

Proof-reading — English in Use. Proof-read to correct the text by identifying the extra words. Procedure: skim read and mark lightly any extra words. Go back to the beginning and read each sentence very carefully. Think what the article is saying; look out for contradictions, illogicalities. The meaning as well as the grammatical forms will help identify the extra words. Remember some lines will be correct. Do the easy ones first, do not waste time on the harder ones until later. Mark the answer only when you are certain.

WHY SOME RELATIONSHIPS HAVE TO END

1	"We had been being best friends since childhood," a young woman told me	**being** 1
2	recently,"and then I started work in the music industry while she	✓ 2
3	stayed on in teaching. Whenever we met, I heard to myself mentioning the	_____ 3
4	names of stars I was working with. Not to show off, neither but because they	_____ 4
5	were becoming an ever-increasing part of my daily life. She'd would get a sort	_____ 5
6	of dazed look, and then a frown of the real disapproval. I could tell she	_____ 6
7	thought I'd sold out and it began to work on my self-confidence. I'd leave	_____ 7
8	her hating myself. But even what could I do? My work was uppermost in my mind	_____ 8
9	and I couldn't afford self doubt. We began to see to each other less and	_____ 9
10	less. Now we exchange Christmas cards. At least we parted without a	_____ 10
11	quarrel." It is nobody's fault when a divergence of thought or career	_____ 11
12	makes it impossible for a close friendship to continue in an honesty: when	_____ 12
13	one friend leaps down to a social, economic or professional level where the	_____ 13
14	other would not be comfortable. I used to know a young actress of great	_____ 14
15	charm and talent and but we were on the edge of becoming great friends when	_____ 15
16	suddenly her career went stratospheric. At first time, I was deeply offended	_____ 16
17	by her cancelled appointments and more than put in out when, as we sat	_____ 17
18	gossiping in a restaurant, except everyone from autograph hounds to Hollywood	_____ 18
19	producers would brush me aside to get going at her.	_____ 19

ENGLISH IN USE   Section C

The new manager in an accounts office decided to put up a list of 'hints' for a better working environment in the office. She made some notes for the secretary to type out in full. Use the notes and write out full sentences for each point.

You must use all the words in the same order as the notes. You may add words and change the form of words where necessary. Look carefully at the example which has been done for you.

1 be tidy put away files book - proper place.

2 want cigarette not smoke here - go outside.

3 got problem someone, not argue speak rationally person explain.

4 still problem speak manager

5 take coffee tea plates canteen not leave office

6 not disturb someone try concentrate

7 try pleasant/friendly chat briefly colleagues - get know each other.

8 try smile least several times day.

How to feel better working in this office

1 _____
2 _____
3 _____
4 _____
5 _____
6 _____
7 _____
8 _____

Problem parents and how to deal with them

What really lies behind parents' behaviour towards their children? By **Louise Hidalgo**

Getting down to basics, here are a few parental profiles to mull over.

1 Parents who were neglected as children themselves often over-compensate by smothering their own offspring with too much attention. When a budding adult is preparing to leave home, their endless dictums about how to behave, how to dress and how to live may also in fact mask a very real need on the part of the parents to remain involved in their children's lives. Emotions can really run high when it comes to that most delicate of subjects — sex. Mixed with the sense of loss at seeing their little child transformed into a nubile or virile young adult can be eddies of envy of their youth and vitality.

2 Then there are the 60's parents, liberal and carefree. They probably wouldn't mind if you don't come home at all, let alone late at night. All well and good, or so you may feel, but it can sometimes be quite consoling to know that someone is waiting at home, worrying about where you are. These kinds of parents often behave like this because they remember themselves, often from bitter experience, how awful it is to have over-strict parents who want to know your every move or lay down the law at every opportunity. In rarer cases, though, the lenience masks indifference and a wish not to get involved. Or perhaps the parents are insecure, and so cut themselves off from any emotional reliance to avoid the terrifying possibility of rejection.

3 Table-thumping, rule-laying parents who won't allow anyone to disagree or disobey sometimes, unfortunately, just enjoy the sense of power. At other times, though, exercising their parental muscle allows them to unload all their own frustrations and thwarted ambitions on to you. They didn't get the promotion at work they were expecting; they're worried financially; they feel they haven't achieved in life what they should have done and now it is too late. Often the temptation to use the family as a sounding-board for all this frustration is just too great.

4 Ever feel you can't do anything right, however hard you try? Well, don't automatically think the fault lies with you. It could be that there are other factors at work behind that disapproving look. These parents may be feeling insecure. They may be lacking in self-esteem. The stresses and strains of everyday life can play straight into any cracks in confidence and come tumbling out as criticism and irritability. If you're the nearest object to hand, get out of the way fast. And then there's the undercurrent of envy. Most parents want only the best for their children, as they probably continually tell you. But when they are feeling unhappy with themselves, when they see their own youth, vitality, even sexuality, slipping away, the urge to diminish someone else's youth can be irresistable. So they may put you down because they find it difficult to cope with their own sense of loss or unhappiness.

5 Everyone goes through fits of depression from time to time, and everyone copes with it in different ways. Some people curl up into a mental and emotional cocoon and don't want to let anyone near. Some people, in contrast, want everyone to know about it. You need advice about a problem and you wouldn't mind some loving support too. But when you approach your parent the response is dismissive, or unreasonably angry. This could just be that they're preoccupied with feeling down and don't have much loving support to spare. So why not just back off for a while and leave them to cope? Families are real power-houses of emotions. When something goes wrong with one part of the balance, such as the marriage, the situation can be highly charged and it is difficult, however hard parents try, to keep it under wraps. And when it's a case of one parent trying to hold on to the marriage, it can be very difficult not to draw the rest of the family into the fray. Parents may unload all their grievances, hurt and rejection onto the children, smothering them with affection and drawing them closer to fill the emotional gap. They may try to exclude the other parent from the relationship, as if to punish or make them jealous. Sometimes, though, this bitterness can be directed at the child, not because of anything they have done or said, but as an outlet for all that pent-up pain.

Questions 1–5

These questions ask you to choose the title for each paragraph. A–H are the possible titles. Choose the one you think is the most appropriate for each paragraph.

1	paragraph 1	A	The Liberal Parent
2	paragraph 2	B	The Enlightened Parent
3	paragraph 3	C	The Uncaring Parent
4	paragraph 4	D	The Exhausted Parent
5	paragraph 5	E	The Domineering Parent
		F	The Depressed Parent
		G	The Overprotective Parent
		H	The Critical Parent

Questions 6–10

These questions ask you to identify the main reasons for parental behaviour which are given in each category. Select your answers for each question from the list A–E.

6	paragraph 1 (1 answer)	A	own childhood
7	paragraph 2 (2 answers)	B	work
8	paragraph 3 (3 answers)	C	marital relationship
9	paragraph 4 (2 answers)	D	own emotional state
10	paragraph 5 (2 answers)	E	personality

WRITING Section B

You are advised to read the question carefully and to write approximately 250 words.

You have been asked to contribute to a local English language newspaper. You have chosen to write a review of a film or television programme which you saw recently. The film or T.V. programme need not have been in English. Include a brief outline of the plot, your opinion of the production and your recommendation to other viewers.

SPEAKING

Written instructions are not normally given to the students. They are included here to familiarise students with the activities.

Phase A

With your partner. Sustain a 'chat' for between two and four minutes exchanging information about your families. Remember this is purely interactive.

Repeat this with one or more other partners.

HELL

10

1 Listen

Listen to this radio
advertisement.

a What is it advertising?
What is the name of the
company?

b Listen again. What five
claims are made? What
does each claim imply
about travelling with
other companies?

2 Discuss

a Look at photo 1. Who
are these people? What
are they doing? Why?
What do you call this
type of passenger?
Where else in the world
do you find them?

b Think of five reasons
why people do this and
five problems they
encounter.

c Look at photo 2. Have
you ever been in this situation? Why do you
think this happens?

d List as many adjectives
as you can to describe
air travel. If you were
writing an advertise-
ment (like the one in
A1) which of these
adjectives would you
use?

1 Read

a Read the title and caption. What do you think the text is about?
b Scan the text and fill in the names of the stations that the train stops at.
c Read more slowly and complete the grid (in note form) for each stage of the journey.
d Draw a sketch to show the layout of the inside of a carriage.

All stops to hell

Edward Pilkington joins commuters on one of the oldest, foulest trains of them all

The calm before the storm... The first commuters board the 07.57 from Orpington in Kent to London's Charing Cross, at the start of their gruelling daily journey into work on one of Britain's most overcrowded lines.

Already hundreds of people from all social classes — City financiers, lawyers, accountants, temps, cleaners and labourers — are streaming into the station. By the time the train pulls out, five minutes late, all the carriages' 82 seats are occupied.

It was clear from the start that this train cannot hope to meet the task ahead. Built in 1954, its carriages were designed for leisurely countryside trips, not for today's massive commuter tide. Passenger capacity is limited because most space is taken up by seats, arranged facing each other in 16 bays, which leaves very little standing room. There is only a thin central aisle and even narrower side aisles leading to wooden-slam doors.

It might be all right if no one gets on after Orpington. Though the seats are full, there is sufficient leg room and just enough space to negotiate a newspaper. But at the first stop, Petts Wood, the deluge begins. A dark line of passengers, two or three deep, greets the train.

It squeaks to a halt, the doors are yanked open and the human horde climbs in, some squashing themselves into seats and others standing in the central aisle, filling it completely.

By now the faces of the passengers have assumed a resigned, gritted-teeth quality which suggests worse to come. As the train pulls into the next stop, Chislehurst, newspapers are folded away and feet tucked under seats in expectation. An even thicker line of anxious commuters pile on in a disorderly scramble.

At the third stop, Elmstead Woods, the real crush is on. People worm their way into any space available, wedged against doors, windows, other bodies, with no room to move their legs and barely enough to turn their heads. The carriage has not straps or bars to hang on to, only iron luggage racks above seats. For people standing in the side aisles this poses a dilemma: they can either stretch over to hold on to the rack, in which case armpits would be thrust above seated passengers' noses, or they can attempt to balance themselves unaided, running the risk of falling into someone's lap. Several people sway against their neighbours as the train bumps and rolls along.

By this time the air has grown hot and stale — an acrid cocktail of body odour, perfume and after-shave, damp clothes and bad breath. The windows are so steamed up that it is impossible to see out.

Apart from physical discomfort, the hardest part of the journey is sheer boredom. There is no question of reading and the few people who talk do so in strictly hushed tones. Most just sit or stand passively, staring in front of them at the nape of a neck or an armpit, or up at the ceiling.

At the penultimate stop, Waterloo East, all pandemonium lets loose. This is an intersection point linking routes into London. About half the carriage struggles to get out pushing past other passengers and through the crowds facing them like a rugby scrum on the platform. As quickly as the carriage empties it is filled again.

Finally the train reaches Charing Cross, now with about 90 people seated and 60 standing. And this was a "good" day — there have only been two cancellations from Orpington this morning. As they pour out of the carriages a faint voice can be heard over the tannoy: "We apologise to passengers for the late arrival of their train. The delay was caused by a signal failure." Nobody listens.

Stations	Condition prevailing
Orpington	*...seats mostly full...*

2 Language

Simple present for narrative description

1 In the text is the writer describing a past event?
2 Is the writer describing one particular day?
3 When do/did these events occur?

What is the effect of writing in the Simple Present?
When might you choose to use the Simple Present?

Adverbials - Time and place markers

These help organise a text. Go through the text above and
underline each time or place adverbial which is used.
For example,   time adverbial *By now ...*

place adverbial *at the third stop ...*

Where are many of them placed? Mark which ones are
time and which ones are place.

Apart from

*Apart from physical discomfort, the hardest part of the
journey is sheer boredom.*

Does this mean:
1 The worst things about the journey are both the
   boredom and the physical discomfort.
2 The journey, while being uncomfortable, is particularly
   hard primarily because of the boredom.
3 The physical discomfort is the hardest part of the
   journey but there is also some boredom.

Rewrite the sentence in a different order. Be careful of the
punctuation. Think about travelling and write three
examples of your own using *apart from* in initial positions.

Comparatives in initial position

As quickly as the carriage empties it is filled again.
Note how *As + adverb/adjective + as* begins the sentence.

It is followed by two clauses. The second is a
contradiction of the first.

Complete these sentences with suitable clauses.
a As fast as she filled the boxes ...
b As hard as he tried he ...
c As tired as they felt ...
d As soon as they left ...

3 Vocabulary

The passage is very rich in vocabulary selected to convey a general feeling of discomfort. What do you feel reading the passage? How would you describe such journeys? How would you feel if you had to do this every day?

One of the ways the author manages to convey the feelings so well is by using words which fall into vocabulary sets. Two sets used here are: lack of space, large numbers of people.

a Look through the text and find any words/phrases which indicate lack of space such as, squash.
Do the same for words/phrases which indicate large numbers of people.

b Using the vocabulary in the sets — look back at the photographs on page 52 and describe the scenes. Talk about your own experiences with daily travel.

Section C

1 Read

a Skim the article very quickly and say in less than 10 words what it is about.

Endpiece
Roy Hattersley

A couple of years ago, I flew home from America on a flight which was not so much delayed as stretched across a whole era of aviation history.

First we were late leaving New York. Then we were held back by adverse winds over the Atlantic. At Heathrow the air traffic was so congested that we circled the capital in increasing gloom. By the time it was our turn to land, fog had engulfed the runways so we were sent back to somewhere over Ockenden. After dawdling for a while above that pleasant town, our petrol began to run out. So we were diverted to Newcastle where, having landed safely, we were forbidden to leave the aircraft. Neither Customs nor Passport Control was ready to deal with the sudden influx of jet setters. Throughout the long night and extended morning the full complement of passengers — with one regrettable exception — remained good humoured. Indeed they were jovial in the manner of guests at a Dickensian Christmas party. They helped the exhausted cabin staff to make hot drinks and, when the instant coffee ran out they passed around the bottled water. At one point singing broke out spontaneously. Hunched on my seat under a blanket that I wore like a wigwam, I might just have managed a chorus of Abide With Me had I not been saving my vocal chords to enquire from a stewardess how long it would be before we were allowed to disembark. "You may not," she told me, "be able to get off here at all. Legally you are still in the air. You may land somewhere else."

Eventually it was decided that we had landed in every sense of the word and flights of steps were manhandled towards the door. As they were pushed into place, years of training switched the stewardess into automatic pilot. "Welcome to Newcastle," she trilled into the public address system. "British Airways hope that you have enjoyed your flight and you will fly with us again." My heart leaped up. That, I felt certain, would spark off the mutiny in which I longed to join. For a moment, the cabin was silent and still. Then the passengers, with one guilty exception, began to applaud.

I cannot recall, in 30 years of morose flying, witnessing a single example of aggressive behaviour whilst in the air. Of course, passengers push and shove, when they are invited to get off. But by then the doors are open and they are no longer in thrall — or no longer whatever else it is that keeps them quiet and obedient.

b Identify the six 'things' which happened to make the journey so terrible.

c How did most people behave? Think of at least three adjectives to describe their feelings. How did the author behave? What do you think he was feeling?

d Imagine yourself on this journey. Think of an adjective to describe how you would have felt at each stage of the journey.

2 Read

Exam

Now read the concluding part of the article. At each blank select the best word from the choice provided.

Peter Ustinov claims to have been a passenger on a Lufthansa flight when, after a period of "turbulence", which (1) ..... the return of passengers to their seats and the fastening of seat belts, the pilot (2)..... the storm-tossed traveller: "You will be pleased to know that I have regained control of the aircraft."

Mr Ustinov marvels at the calm of the (3)..... specimens that sat around him. I, at least, realise that they were catatonic with fear. What I cannot understand is tranquility in the face of constant (4)...... When — having declined food and drink, switched on the overhead light to (5)..... for the cabin being darkened in preparation for the movie, conditioned myself to the snoring gentleman on my right, (6) ..... down to read and write, I am politely asked to remove my bag from under my knees to the locker above my head and to store away my table — it seems to me that hysteria is the only decent reaction. And there is only one decent reply. Beam me down Scottie.

1	a	drove	b	justified	c	examined	d	advised
2	a	explained	b	said	c	addressed	d	warned
3	a	threatening	b	dangerous	c	enraged	d	endangered
4	a	inconvenience	b	inconsistent	c	conviviality	d	annoyance
5	a	balance	b	compensate	c	maker	d	dispense
6	a	settled	b	got	c	sank	d	lay

Section D

1 Listen

Two people, Bruce and Sean, give short descriptions of their own particularly bad journeys.

a Listen to each description and state in what country the journey took place. Say in a few words the real reason why each journey was so terrible.

b Listen again to Bruce. Why did he go? What caused his illness? What transport did he use? How did he feel about the journey?

c Listen again to Sean. What transport did he use? What was in the back? What was the driver's problem? What was Sean's problem? What did he do? How did Sean feel a moment later?

2 Speak

Have you ever experienced a particularly bad journey?
Think about the journey. Why was it so terrible? What
happened? Make notes, use some of the new vocabulary
from this unit. Do not write sentences. Try to speak for
approximately one minute.

3 Write

Exam

The two passages (page 55 and 56) are both examples of
descriptive travel writing. Descriptive writing is very rich
in vocabulary, particularly verbs and adjectives.

Write a description of either a habitual journey, as in *All
Stops to Hell* using primarily the Simple Present, or one
particular journey, as in *Endpiece* using primarily the
Simple Past.

Step 1   Think of the particular feelings you want to con-
         vey and brainstorm a list of vocabulary items.
         Some you can organise in sets. You may not use all
         of them, they serve as a bank.

Step 2   Make notes, organised chronologically, about the
         events.

Step 3   Decide how to use examples of the following
         patterns:
         as + adverb/adjective + as   apart from

Step 4   Use time and place adverbials to organise your text
         and write a draft.

Step 5   Go back through the text and make adjustments,
         adding and changing words to bring out the
         'feeling/mood' you wish to convey. Correct any
         errors.

Step 6   Swap your draft with a partner and try to help
         them identify any errors.

Step 7   When you are satisfied with the passage write a
         final copy 100 to 150 words long.

Learner Skills

- using different strategies to
  comprehend a text
- organising vocabulary in sets
- intensive listening
- giving descriptive accounts both
  spoken and written

Exam Skills

	Listening
A1	listening for facts
	Speaking
A2	analysing and interpreting a photograph
	Reading
B1	extracting facts from text
	Speaking
B3 b	describing a scene in a photograph
	English in Use
C2	multiple choice selection of
Exam	vocabulary
	Writing
D 3	descriptive writing
Exam	

HEAVEN

11

1 Speak

Exam

Work in pairs. Student A should look at photo 3 on page 171 and Student B should look at photo 7 on page 172. Study the pictures, then describe and discuss your picture with your partner.

Prepare a short summary of your conclusions. Discuss your conclusions with the class.

2 Listen

You are going to listen to a description of a journey in the Bolivian Andes. Look at the headings below and as you listen make notes under each:

where the journey takes place
the means of transport
the passengers
the physical environment
the narrator's feelings

Discuss and compare your notes.

3 Write

On the right is an excerpt from the Bolivian journey.

a Listen again and read the transcript in Box A simultaneously. Now look at Box B. This is a written version of the same part of the story. Compare the two versions. Comment on: the sentences, the words, repetition. Discuss the ways in which they are different.

A … then on the very top right in the middle of nowhere these barren empty, dry open spaces and there we stopped we stopped to let somebody out and he climbed out with all his gear he was carrying… set off into the distance of what looked like nowhere I mean there was no habitation nothing to be seen from where we were. Anyway then the lorry started off again and off we went …

B At the very top of the cliff was very dry, empty, barren, open land and there, in the middle of nowhere, the train stopped. It had stopped to allow someone to get out. He climbed out carrying all his belongings and set off into the distance of what appeared to be nowhere. There was no habitation or building to be seen. After a moment the 'lorry' was started up again and we continued.

Exam **b** Study the excerpt in Box C. Listen again. Complete the written version of this section in Box D by adding one or two words in each blank. The first one is done for you.

C ... there was one point I counted ten mountain ranges you could see from the peaks we were travelling on you could actually count ten ranges of mountains heading off into the distance and the valleys got richer and richer and warmer we came to subtropical sort of areas. We travelled like this for four or five hours and there was an overall descent and of course dark comes very quickly there. By the time dark was coming we were descending into green rich vegetation. It was thick and it was getting damp and a lot warmer ...

D At one time, from our vantage point __high on__ the peaks we travelled along, I was _____ count a _____ of ten mountain ranges disappearing off into the distance. Then gradually the valleys _____ and richer and, notably warmer. They were in _____ regions. We travelled through these regions for about four or five hours all the _____ descending. Darkness arrives very suddenly there and by the time _____ fell we were _____ into the _____ vegetation and the air was becoming damp and considerably warmer.

Section B

1 Read

Exam The British newspaper, *The Observer*, organises an annual travel writers' competition. The following entry won its author a place amongst the six finalists in 1989.

Read and fill in the gaps with one of the options from the list. You will not use all the options.

Silvery fish on a line

Luke Blair

In the compartment next to mine there were two old men, and, wrapped in paper on the table between them, a large, silvery fish.

1	

It was a poignant introduction to the longest railway line in the world, but as T.S. Eliot once said, 'the first condition of understanding a foreign country is to smell it'.

The trans-Siberian railway is about 6,000 miles long and stretches across the Soviet Union from the Gulf of Finland to the Sea of Japan.

I was travelling only a quarter of its length from Novosibirsk on the West Siberian Plain to Irkutsk at the foothills of the Mongolian Plateau and, on the whole, had a remarkably comfortable journey.

2	

Most of the snow had melted when I travelled across Siberia in April and the landscape was a bleak expanse of yellow grass, black earth and vast, leafless forests of skeletal birch trees.

3	

The scattered villages of toy-like wooden cabins looked out of place in this hostile environment, with their brightly-painted window frames and lacy, finely-carved eaves.

My fellow passengers appeared to relish the warmth of the train, many remaining in their sleeping-berths throughout the two-day journey.

Our carriage attendant, who had brought us tea from the built-in samovar when we first boarded, was made of sterner stuff. The perfect stereotype of Soviet femininity, she was broad, muscular and when she was not arguing with her husband in their cramped compartment at the end, she was sweeping the corridor carpet.

4	

The waiter in the dining car was a different matter. Grinning from ear to ear, he served up each meal in filthy hands with an expression that suggested inordinate pride in his offerings.

5	

But we did have caviar — bright orange bubbles of it served with hard boiled eggs — as the dining car rattled through the birch forests.

6	

Luke Blair, 24, is a journalist in Ipswich.

Exam Strategies

Gapped text — Reading.
Sections of the text are blanked out and you have a list of options to select from. One option will not be used. Procedure: skim read the text and the options. Mark any that seem obvious. Read the sentences before and after. Try out the options. If you think one is correct, check that you can eliminate the others. If you cannot find the answer, move on. Do not worry about working in order – correct completion of a gap will make it easier to complete others.

A It took half the journey and a generous measure of vodka from some Scottish companions before she traded smiles with us.

B What the ventilation system lacked in keeping the carriage free of fishy odours it made up for by keeping us warm.

C Winding its way steadily across plains and mountains, the Trans-Siberian railway takes the traveller on an unforgettable journey.

D The door was ajar and a peculiar odour filled the modern, East German-built carriage.

E The two old men in the compartment next door did not join us for meals, but I noticed when we reached our destination that the fish had disappeared.

F In fact the glutinous meat, menthol-flavoured drink and pickled vegetables were swallowed with some stoicism.

G The plains seemed scorched by the climate of extremes in which temperatures in the seventies in summer plummet to well below zero in the winter.

2 Vocabulary

Mark the vocabulary you do not know. Very often you can guess the 'gist' meaning of a word (in context) simply by applying logic, and you do not have to understand exactly what it is to be able to comprehend the passage.

a What is the meaning of each of the following in the text? What helped you? Can you identify how you guessed the meaning?

1 finely-carved eaves
   a part of the houses
   b part of the train
   c a type of landscape

2 to relish
   a to enjoy
   b to hate
   c to suffer

3 samovar
   a sort of oven
   b a sort of tea-making machine
   c a sort of kettle

4 birch
   a a colour
   b a type of stick
   c a type of tree

b Look back at the vocabulary you marked earlier and try to understand something about each word from the context. Make a list of any items you have no idea about.

c Choose three adjectives and three verbs from the text whose meaning you did not know before. For each adjective think of at least three other nouns that you could describe in this way. For each verb think of a different context in which it could be used.

3 Speak

Work in groups of four. Imagine you went on this journey and each take a different section of the text.

paras. 1–6   paras. 9–10
paras. 7–8   paras. 11–13

Prepare to give a spoken account of your section. You will probably take many more words. You will repeat words, change the order and will use short phrases, not long complex sentences. Listen and help each other as you try to give a good natural account.

Section C

1 Discuss
Work with the same group. The six finalists of the
Observer Competition were all sent to the Phillipines to
prepare their final story. Imagine you are organising a similar competition. You have six finalists and you must
decide where, when and how you would send them in
order to produce interesting, entertaining articles. Report
your decisions to the class.

2 Task
You are to take part in a similar type of competition. In
this competition you have to give both a spoken and a
written account of an interesting journey.

Step 1 Decide on your journey. It may be one you have
really experienced or it could be one you have read
about in a newspaper, magazine, or a travel book,
or you can invent one. In any case you will
describe the journey in the first person.

Step 2 Make outline notes for your talk which should last
about 1–2 minutes. Give your talk.

Step 3 Write your own version of the journey from the
notes for your talk. Write a draft version first,
swap, proof-read, correct and then write the final
copy 120 to 180 words long.

Learner Skills

- working with spoken and written description
- listening for specific information
- making notes from listening
- negotiating and exchanging ideas and opinions
- guessing words in context
- developing awareness of collocation

Exam Skills

	Speaking
A1	working out the relationship
Exam	between photographs
	English in Use
A3b	register rewriting
Exam	
	Reading
B1	completion of gapped text
Exam	
	English in Use
B2	guessing meaning of words
	in context
	Speaking
C1	reporting on discussions
	Speaking
C2	long turn speaking
	Writing
C2	writing descriptive travel
	passage

REALITY

12

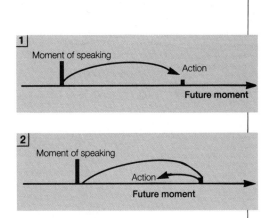

---

1 Task
What details other than dates does a travel agent need to know to make a booking for a client? Make a list.

2 Listen
Listen to this conversation between a travel agent and a client. Imagine you are the travel agent and take down all the necessary details. Use your headings if you like. What details do you still need? How will you get the information?

3 Write
Write the fax to send to São Paulo.

4 Listen
Listen to the subsequent telephone conversation with the client and complete the list you started above of necessary details about the trip.

5 Language
Future continuous and future perfect

a Listen again and complete these excerpts from the second conversation.

1 There's not any choice. You ... a coach. (catch)
2 We ... overnight I presume. (travel)
3 That way I ... two full days there before moving on. (have)
4 I ... plenty of time by then to look through the guide books. (have)
5 I think ... that actually. (take care of)

Which of the sentences indicates
• completion of something by a certain time?
• personal future intention?
• a statement of fixed plans

b The two tenses can both be represented by the time lines. One of them showing what is happening at a given moment in the future. The other showing the past of the future. Which diagram matches which definition and which tense?

1

Moment of speaking

Action

Future moment

2

Moment of speaking

Action

Future moment

6 Write

Exam

Using all the details you have noted and the faxed reply from Brazil, complete the letter below from the travel agent to the client. The letter is to confirm th details of the trip.

Step 1 Organise your information in a logical order. Think how best to present the information.

Step 2 Think of suitable sentences to continue and to finish the letter.

Step 3 Write the letter being careful to select appropriate vocabulary. Remember this is formal and informative. Proof-read. Write the final copy 120 to 180 words long.

TRAVEL BUG - TRAVEL EXPERTS
17 Hawthorn Avenue
Ealing W6 8QT

J Crispin Esq
47 Hanover Gardens
London   W6 7BJ
                    25 October 1991

Dear Mr Crispin

Re: Trip to Rio, Iguaçu and Buenos Aires

It gives me pleasure to include details of your itinerary.

Yours sincerely

Ann Holt

Ann Holt
Manager

FAX MESSAGE

To: Ann Holt (Travel Bug)
From: Carlos Boffini
Pages: 1

Subject: Details of trip - Rio, Iguaçu, Buenos Aires

Hotel: Hotel Iguaçu (4 star), Foz de Iguaçu, Brazil. Single room with bath and breakfast 350,000 Cruzerios/£50 per night. Dinner and lunch a la carte menu from £10.

Travel: Rio to São Paulo - suggest shuttle flight leaving the city airport at regular intervals. Can be included on transatlantic flight ticket. Allow 2.5 hours from leaving Rio to be at coach station in S.P. to check in.

Travel: S.P. to Iguaçu — best available overland is luxury coach ... cost £15 length of journey 15 hours departure 19:00 arrival 10:00.

Travel: Iguaçu to Posadas/Buenos Aires — coach to Posadas (recommended visit to Jesuit ruins) - cost £5 - afternoon service. Overnight coach to BA - cost £20.

1 Read

Today there is a great deal of debate about the relative advantages and disadvantages of road versus rail transport.

a Skim read this article published on 24 November 1989 and say
1 what the relationship is between transport and the environment.
2 what the EEC was/is intending to do about these issues.
3 what EEC stands for.

Exam **b** Select appropriate headings for each paragraph from the following list.

Rail Movement   EEC Plans   Example Case
Historical Perspective   Interest in Railways

2 Language

Prediction

Three different ways of predicting the future are used in this passage. Identify the pattern used in the following cases.
1 Traffic in the next decade.
2 The Channel Tunnel.
3 Europe's rail networks.

3 Speak

Say what you think will happen to transport:
1 in your region in the next 25 years.
2 around the world by the year 2001.

Think of at least five points to make for each topic.

Beyond the Frontier Spirit

As the frontiers of Europe are breached on the way to 1992, the environmental crisis created by the community's transport policies, or lack of them, continues to deepen. During the seventies and early eighties, investment throughout western Europe in roads and railways fell. When economies started to boom the problems for the environment started to accelerate. Car ownership took off, despite the fact that the internal combustion engine is the most potent pollutant in Europe.

In the next decade, there will be a further acceleration of travel and traffic. Southern England has some of the worst transport problems in Europe and the Channel Tunnel is set to make the links with Europe even closer and the environmental problems caused by high-speed rail links and increased traffic even worse.

Across Europe, there is renewed interest in developing the rail ways, exemplified by this week's announcement by the European transport commissioner that Europe's rail networks are to be thrown open to private enterprise. But repeated attempts by the EC to introduce a Common Transport Policy throughout Europe have been frustrated by the Council of Ministers who prefer to keep transport investment to themselves.

This week's meeting in Paris of European Community transport ministers has for the first time devoted a session to transport and the environment. On the agenda were problems of traffic management and questions of infrastructure, as well as an attempt to introduce economic incentives to reduce vehicle emissions.

4 Read

The following cuttings were all taken from articles supporting either rail or road development.

a Skim read them and divide them accordingly.

Exam **b** When writing an article to support one side of the argument there is the possibility of either
- being positive about cars and/or negative about railways

or
- being positive about railways and/or negative about cars.

Study the extracts and say which of those techniques is used in each one.

A The car is not dependent on public transport's incompetent managers and obstructive trades unions. It is impossible to imagine any type of bus or train service that does not keep passengers waiting at lonely locations at night.

B The situation gets worse in the Alps. Massive damage has been done to the tree cover from the concentration of exhaust gases and the risk of avalanches in winter and landslips in spring has been severely increased.

C Apart from the obvious jam caused by accidents and road repairs, many of the worst begin on urban feeder roads built in the 1960s and 1970s. During the morning rush-hour the car parks fill up and the queue of motorists tails back to these distributor roads. The junctions jam, the queue reaches back to the urban motorways where the exit lanes jam and then, as traffic can't leave them, the motorways themselves jam.

D Unlike the bus, train tube it goes from where you a to where you want to be, wh you want to, and can carry y and your baggage far m comfortably.

E In short, transport for the public is not found only in mass transit organised collectively. The car provides real public transport. It is more convenient than other inflexible forms, and promotes freedom.

5 Language
Criticising

The following patterns (from the texts) are all used to criticise.

Apart from this there is also that. (in addition)

Unlike the ... the ... does (the ... does not)

It is impossible to imagine ... that does not do (they all do this)

Use these three patterns to write critical comments about air and sea transport.

6 Listen

Listen to these people express their opinions on issues of transport.

Exam

Complete the chart to show which system they support or if they are neutral. Tick the appropriate box.

Which speakers hold the strongest views? What tells you that?

speaker	1	2	3	4	5	6	7	8
supports roads								
supports rail								
neutral								

Section C

1 Discuss

Hold an organised debate with observers. Divide into groups of A's, B's and C's.

a A's prepare as many arguments as they can in favour of trains and expansion of the rail network. B's prepare arguments in favour of road transport and expansion of interconnecting motorways.
C's are journalists observing the debate and need to discuss the organisation of their observation. For example, headings for notes, etc.

b Re-arrange the class into groups each with one C and an equal number of A's and B's. A's and B's discuss and debate the issues. Try to convince each other of the benefits of their particular system. The C in each group takes notes on the discussion and any conclusions reached.

c The C from each group must give a report to the class.

d Now discuss the issues giving your own personal opinion.

2 Write

Exam

Prepare a written report on the discussion you had. This should be a group effort with one final copy given to the teacher.

Step 1 Study C's notes and select the information you want to use.

Step 2 Categorise the information into the various arguments. Those in favour or against the conclusion.

Step 3 Individually write drafts of different sections. Try to use some of the 'written opinion language' studied in Section B.

Step 4 Proof-read for errors and make adjustments to the passage.

Step 5 Write a final copy of 150 to 200 words long.

Exam Skills

	Listening
A2/4	extracting specific facts
	Writing
A6	analysing information and
Exam	writing text
	Reading
B1	selecting paragraph heading
Exam	*Reading*
B4b	interpreting attitude of text
Exam	*Listening*
B6	interpreting tone and meaning
Exam	*Speaking*
C1c	reporting on discussion
	Writing
C2	writing reports
Exam	

Learner Skills

- working with factual information
- formal letter and report writing
- analysing information in a text
- working with purpose and tone of text
- understanding viewpoints
- debating

EXAM SECTION

You will hear a Radio Clyde travel report giving details of all travel problems on one day. As you listen you must fill in the information for Questions A–I. You will hear this piece twice.

Travel Report

Rail	Number of cancellations	1
	Time of trains cancelled	A _____
	Alternative train times	8.31 and B _____

Road	Total number of problems	6
	Congested road numbers	M73 C _____ D _____ M77
	Cause on M73 and one	
	section of M77	E _____

Air	***Flight from***	***flight to***	***latest information***
	Glasgow	Vancouver	departure delayed
	New York/Boston	Glasgow	arriving F _____
	G _____	Glasgow	arriving 20 minutes early
	Glasgow	H _____	departure delayed
	Manchester	Glasgow	arriving I _____

Exam Strategies

Completing facts/diagram — Listening. A diagram or grid contains some information; you have to complete the missing information where indicated. Procedure: study the diagram carefully and make sure you understand what information is missing. As you listen note that information (on scrap paper). On second listening make changes/add information. Fill in the answer sheet in ink.

SPEAKING   *Phase C/D*

Look at the two pictures (your partner has the same pictures).
Discuss with your partner which is the best way to travel and why. You must either reach agreement or agree to disagree. Make sure you understand your partner's opinion.
You must be prepared to give a report on your discussion/decision after three to four minutes.

Exam Strategies

Phase C — Speaking.
You will have a stimulus: a quotation, picture, etc, which raises a particular issue. You ideally want to talk with your partner about the issue for 3–4 minutes. Procedure: begin the discussion by clarifying what is said/what the issue is. Then start to express your opinion and/or ask your partner what they think. Try to discuss all aspects of the issue. The communication / negotiation with your partner is very important. Remember the examiners are not interested in your opinion but in your ability to express your opinion. You must either reach agreement or agree to disagree.

IN SPACE

13

1 Task

Can you answer these questions?

1 Which is the smallest planet?
2 Who/what was the first living being in space?
3 Which planet was discovered most recently?
4 When we look at the stars, do we see what is happening (at that moment)?
5 Who invented the telescope?
6 Who first landed on the moon and when?

2 Read

Now read this newspaper article and see if you were right.

3 Language

Passive reporting verbs

a Listen to these comments. Which do you agree with?

Comment

	1	2	3	4	5	6
Agree						
Disagree						

In 2 and 3 who is *they*? In numbers 5 and 6 what word is understood to follow *many* and *some*?

b When we are talking about an opinion/thought/belief we can use this pattern:
Noun/pronoun + reporting verb + *that*.

We can however reorganise the sentence using the Passive and beginning with *It*. So number 1 becomes:
It is said that Galileo invented the telescope.

c Listen again to each utterance and then write an alternative beginning with *It*.

Coo, fancy that

• Pluto is the last discovered planet of our Galaxy. It was first spotted in 1930.

• The smallest planet is Mercury. It has a diameter of 4880 kilometers. (The Earth has a diameter of 12750km)

• The first Moon landing was in July 1969, by the American astronauts Armstrong and Aldrin.

• The stars are so far away from the Earth that the light they are giving out needs several years to reach us.

So when we watch the stars in the sky we see what happened there some years ago. The stars we watch may not exist at all any more.

• A Dutch spectacle-maker discovered the telescope in 1608 and not Galileo Galilei as it is always said.

Galileo just improved this invention and used it for the observation of planets.

• The dog Laika was the first living being in space. He "travelled" in the Soviet satellite Sputnik 2 in November 1957.

4 Speak

a Divide into A's, B's and C's. Work in groups of 3 or 4 with others of the same letter. Groups of A's take topic 1, B's take topic 2 and C's take topic 3. Discuss and make a note of the most commonly held beliefs about your topic.

b Work with a different group composed of an A, a B and a C. Report on your topic and exchange ideas. Use the *It* pattern when you can.

Topics
1 Life on other planets
2 Extra-terrestrial visitors to Earth in ancient history
3 The value of space exploration today

Section B

A Voyage of no return

The space mission Voyager 2 recently passed Neptune. Imogen Edwards-Jones reports on the findings of the satellite which has boldly gone where man cannot.

1 Read

What is a voyage of no return?
What is Voyager 2? Why can we not pass Neptune?
List fifteen nouns that you think will be included in the article.

2 Read

Exam

As you read tick off any of the nouns you predicted.

a For each paragraph 1–9 select the most appropriate heading from this list:

Voyager's Journey
The Limits
Super Active Neptune
Shakespeare's Characters
Our Society Encapsulated
Possibilities of Life
Great Discoveries
The Jupiter Discovery
New Moons
NASA's Hopes
The Aims
Voyager's Achievement

1 When Voyager 2 flew past Neptune on 24–25 August 1989, only 1.4 seconds behind schedule and travelling at a speed of 40,000 mph, it was finally able to transmit pictures of the planet back to Earth. For NASA it was the culmination of the 12-year mission of the satellite which began from Earth in September 1977.

2 On its way to Neptune, Voyager 2 also passed Jupiter in July 1979, Saturn in November 1980, and Uranus in January 1986. It is hoped that the satellite will go on to reach Pluto in 2015, where it will eventually run out of power and drift into outer space. However, the discoveries the satellite has already made are probably far in excess of what the scientists at NASA in Pasadena, California ever expected.

3 For instance, Jupiter was previously thought not to have any rings, but this was proved false by the Voyager mission. A thin flat ring of particles was discovered surrounding Jupiter which means that it now joins Saturn and Uranus to become the third planet in the solar system known to possess a planetary ring system. This leaves Neptune as the only member of the group of giant planets without a known ring.

4 Two new moons were also discovered by Voyager 2, which makes the known total 15. They have all been named after Shakespearian characters. The two new moons have been called Cordelia and Orphelia. Volcanic activity detected on Miranda and Ariel, two other moons, seems to defy what scientists originally thought, that the further away from the sun the planet, the less active it is. In fact, it appears that the reverse is true. But then Voyager 2 produced a great many intriguing new discoveries; on the surface of Miranda, white cliffs that stand 20km high (twice the height of Everest) have been found.

5 But it was perhaps on Neptune and its surrounding satellites that the most exciting discoveries were made. The first colour images of the moon Titan were received, showing Titan to be pink and with a blue layer on top. Its atmosphere appears to contain the building blocks for the formation of life.

6 Neptune itself is blue because its atmosphere is made of nitrogen and also has 1,500 mph winds whistling across the planet. The planet has 10 mile high geysers that spurt out nitrogen and leave snowy deposits around the vents. These geysers were the most important discovery made about the planet, and they were not identified until seven weeks after all the data from Neptune had been assimilated. All this activity on Neptune now completely disproves the old theory that the planets furthest from the sun are the most inactive and boring.

7 Probably the greatest impediment to space travel is its expense and the fact that often it may serve no immediate, practical purpose. NASA justifies the great expense of space exploration with the three aims laid down in the Voyager mission. They are:

1. To discover other life forms.
2. To discover another home for man, and to see if any other planet could be of use to man from the point of view of natural resources.
3. To try to discover why and more precisely how the world began.

8 Ironically, none of these aims were achieved on the Voyager missions so far. However, many more facets of our solar system were discovered. Some believe that man cannot travel any further until our present technology is much improved. It will not be until 'warp-mode' is invented that man himself will be able to go to Neptune on holiday.

9 Until then we will have to rely on 'them out there' to contact us. But at least if Voyager 2 were discovered on her travels after she passes Pluto there is a wealth of information on board to interest anyone. It includes: most of the worlds' languages on tape, the sound of a baby crying and of a hyena, plus photographs of children and the Golden Gate Bridge. Let's hope it doesn't put them off!

b From the information contained in this passage answer these questions with one of the options in the box. Some of the choices will be used more than once.

1 Which planets are now known to have rings?

(3) _____ _____ _____

2 Which will be the last planet we will receive data on?
(1) _____

3 Where did they find proof that distant planets are in fact very active? (1) _____

4 Where else has volcanic activity been identified?
(2) _____ _____

5 Where have unusual land formations been found?
(1) _____

6 Which large planet has no rings? (1)_____

Cordelia Jupiter Pluto Saturn Ariel
Uranus Miranda Neptune

3 Language
Passive voice

a Consider these questions.
  1 Why do we use the Passive Voice?
  2 In what type of texts can we find it?

b Underline all the examples of the passive voice in the text (pp71–72). Work in pairs and name the tense used in each example. Compare your work with others.

c Look at these sentences from the text. Can you rewrite them using *It is/was said/thought* … etc.
  1 Jupiter was previously thought not to have any rings.
  2 Some believe that man can not travel any further …

d Find the example in paragraph 2 using the *it* pattern. Rewrite it in a different way.

4 Write

Exam

Use the following notes as the basis and write another paragraph about Voyager. Remember this is written scientific style. Use the Passive as appropriate. You must use all the words in the same order as in the notes. You may add words and change the form of words as necessary.

From a photo / a new satellite of Neptune / total now 17. / proposed name Adestrea / Adestrea a nymph / Greek mythology/ nursed the infant Zeus. / 4 of the other satellites / size equal to Earth. / Io, Europe, Ganymede and Calisto / not yet household names / add to list / earth-size planets / solar system. / Voyager mission / photograph satellites / close-up / enable scientists / observe details / first time.

5 Vocabulary

a Using your own knowledge and information from the passage, find appropriate words to complete these phrases.

1 Satellites ... pictures back to Earth.
2 Space ... is very expensive.
3 The different ... in any atmosphere.
4 Rings ... the planet.
5 DNA is a building block for the ... of life.
6 Planets belong to particular ... system.
7 The Voyager ... have been vital.
8 Aims must be ... before you begin.

b For each of the above words think of related nouns, verbs, or adjectives, for example: exploration, to explore, explorative.

6 Task

a Work in small groups. Decide on a list of 20 items you would have placed in Voyager's capsule. Remember the idea is to convey as much information about our world and society as possible. You may include any of the items which really were sent.

b Compare your list with another group's and work with them until you produce one list of 20 items between you.

Learner Skills

- expressing doubt
- giving indirect opinion
- word building
- negotiating and agreeing with others

Exam Skills

	Speaking
A4b	reporting on discussion
	English in Use
B2a/b	title selection and multiple match
Exam B4	*English in Use* constructing text from notes
Exam B6	*Speaking* negotiating skills

OUR INHERITANCE

14

Section A

1 Speak
Exchange your views/opinions on 'How the Earth was formed'. What do you believe?

2 Listen
Listen to an astronomer give one explanation as to how the Earth was formed. Complete the following statements using one, or more than one word per blank.

Exam

1 ___It was one thought___ that the Earth was the centre of the Universe.

2 There are approximately _____ stars in our galaxy.

3 After the Big Bang the Universe was filled ___with radiation___.

4 The sun is not the only star ___in the universe___.

5 Today galaxies are still ___rushing away from___ each other.

6 The big question is will there be ___an end___ to this?

7 One possibility is the opposite of the Big Bang, in effect ___the big crunch___.

8 However scientists today ___cannot say___ what will happen.

Section B

1 Vocabulary
a For each of the following verbs think of a substitute : to erode, to form, to erupt, to deposit.

b Build other words from the ones above.

c Mark which you would be likely to see in a geography text book.

2 Read
Different natural forces change the shape of the Earth. List the major elemental forces mentioned in the text. Check your list with two others.

S ince its creation, the planet Earth has never ceased to change and the natural forces which cause physical change are powerful and usually beyond our control. Consider the damage caused by hurricane winds; the destruction wrought by an earthquake; the erosion of cliffs constantly battered by waves; the flooded valleys and plains deluged by monsoon rain and the awesome primeval force of volcanoes. After a typhoon or an earthquake has hit a region it is never the same again ...

3 Language
Noun phrases and relative clauses

A noun phrase usually has a noun (or pronoun) as its head-word. It may be preceded by a determiner (*the*, *that*), or a quantifier (*some*, *hundreds*) and/or adjectives. Look at the following examples:

Humanity (one word only)
Some twentieth-century human beings (several words)
Humans who didn't live in caves (with a subsidiary clause)

A noun phrase can be followed or preceded by a verb phrase.

a Identify the noun phrases in the text. Identify the part of speech of each word in each phrase. Note the relevant verb phrase to which it is related.

b What words are omitted in this noun phrase?
  … the damage caused by hurricane winds.

  We call this a reduced-relative clause. It could have been written:
  … the damage which was caused by hurricane winds.

  Which other noun phrases in the text belong to this type? Rewrite each example with a full defining relative clause.

c Rewrite the following noun phrases as reduced relative clauses:
  1 The floods which were caused by heavy rainfall have …
  2 The people who were living there have …
  3 International rescue teams who have been sent to the region are …
  4 Further rainfall which was predicted has …
  5 Certain areas where trees had been planted did not …
  6 Money and supplies which the International community have sent are …

4 Discuss

a List all the natural forces you can think of on the board. Choose one of the forces. Exchange any knowledge you have about this force. What it is? How does it operate? What effects does it cause?

b Explain everything you possibly can about 'your force' and try to answer any questions. Listen and ask questions about the other forces.

c With the class collect all the information in note form under relevant headings on the board.

5 Listen

Listen to this group of people discussing what they know about natural forces.

1 List the forces they discuss.

2 Note down any 'new' information (not on the board).

3 Do you think that they are wrong on any point/s? If so, which? Why?

6 Language

Expressing doubt

If we have doubt about the truth of a point, we indicate this with particular words and patterns said with appropriate intonation.

a There are many instances during the taped discussion when the speakers express their doubt about some fact. Listen to these excerpts and note the examples.

b Think of as many different patterns you can use (including the ones from the discussion). Listen to the tape and see if you have included all these patterns. Make example sentences of 'new' patterns.

7 Speak

Write the name of a physical geography topic you only know a little about on a piece of paper. Put the pieces of paper together. Choose one topic at a time and say what you can about it. Include what you are certain of, what you think is true and what might be true. Practise using the different ways to indicate your doubt/certainty.

8 Write

Exam

Write a passage giving information on one of the elemental forces.

Step 1 Collect all the information you have about one of the forces.

Step 2 Now organise that information into a paragraph. Begin with the general and move to the specific facts.

Step 3 Write the draft paragraph. Make sure you use different types of noun phrases, include at least one reduced relative clause, and make use of the passive.

Step 4 Proof-read the paragraph, then write a final copy 150 to 200 words long.

Section C

1 Speak

a Look at the world map. Using the same symbols mark
more examples of the following on your map.
mountain ranges   rivers   ice-caps
lakes   deserts   forests

Do not discuss this with anyone and do not show your
map to anyone.

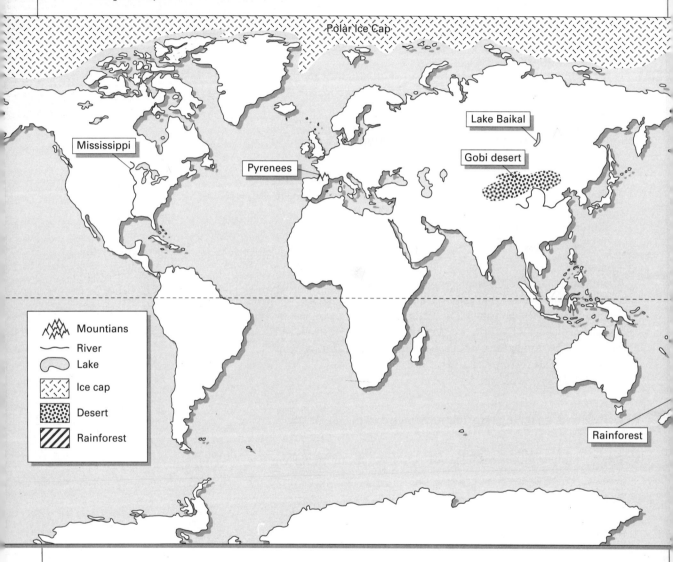

Polar Ice Cap

Mississippi

Pyrenees

Lake Baikal

Gobi desert

Rainforest

Mountians
River
Lake
Ice cap
Desert
Rainforest

Exam   **b** Now sit back to back with a partner. Exchange all the
information you have, marking everything on your map
until your maps are identical.

c Now change partners and repeat the process.

2 Listen

Exam

Have you ever seen either of the geographical formations shown in the photos? If so, where? The first is an example of what is called a stack and the second is of a coastal spit.

a Listen to the explanation of how the stack is formed and label as many features on the diagram as possible.

b Listen to the explanation of how a coastal spit is formed and draw a rough diagram. Draw it as if you were looking down from above and make sure you include the waves, the longshore drift, the spit, and the bay.

c Compare your diagram with a partner. Make any changes. Listen again to both explanations and make any adjustments. Agree on a final version of each.

high tide

low tide

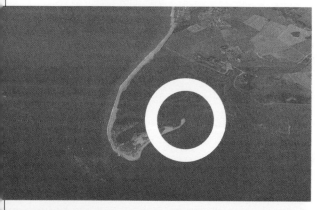

Learner Skills

- exchanging information, opinions and beliefs
- understanding talks on scientific subjects
- implying and expressing doubt

Exam Skills

A1	*Speaking* exchanging information	
B4	*Speaking* exchanging information	
B5	*Listening* listening for specific facts	
B8 Exam	*Writing* formal scientific writing	
C1 Exam	*Speaking* information gap exchanging information	
C2 Exam	*Listening* labelling/completing diagrams	

OUR INFLUENCE

15

Section   A

1 Read
Look at the headlines. What do you expect each article to be about?

1 **Can polar bears tread water?**

2 Language
First and second conditional revision

a Say what will happen if:
Low-lying islands/countries disappear beneath the sea.
We eat mutant vegetables.
Frost prevents oranges growing in Florida/Spain/Sicily.
Polar bears are unable to swim.

b Do you think the ice-caps really will melt? If you think any of the above are unlikely, how can you express that? If you think any of them are certain to happen, how can you express that? Give examples.

c Write down three things that will happen *if we don't* do something about global warming.
Now rewrite the sentences but replace *if we don't* with a different phrase still expressing the same concept.

2 **Freak weather in Florida—it's almost scary.**

3 **Everest clean up climb**

3 Listen
Listen to an account of each of the articles.

a First listen to see if your expectations are confirmed. What photographs would you place beside these articles?

Exam b Listen again and say if the following statements are True or False.
1 Because of the melting ice-cap, sea levels have risen 50 centimetres.
2 The article really asks what will happen to polar bears when there is no ice-cap.
3 The conference was arranged by countries consisting of small islands.
4 Geological activity will cause the islands to sink.
5 Near Chernobyl, trees and vegetables are growing to extreme proportions.
6 Humans are being born with deformities.
7 Extreme cold in Florida was predicted.
8 The fruit trees were not affected.
9 Climbers have left rubbish all over Mount Everest.
10 Volunteers have gone to tidy up.

4 **...As mutant vegetables appear.**

5 **Small islands fear from global warming.**

1 Read

a As you read the following text, list the environmental issues the author (indirectly) mentions?

b Is this text written in a serious manner? If yes, what is the author's opinion of 'green' issues? If no, describe her approach?

c What do the following words refer to?
it (line 7)   *we* (line 8)   *it* (line 10)

people (line 19)   *it* (line 24)   *they* (line 27)

it (line 28)   *it* (line 30)   *it* (line 35)   *it* (line 39)

we (line 42)

2 Vocabulary

a Find the compound nouns in the text which mean:
1 something which freshens the air
2 a type of tin which sprays using gases for pressure
3 a layer of ozone
4 gases, etc, which are expelled from a car through the exhaust
5 rubbish which has been subject to radiation

b What do the following mean in the passage:
1 dumped — left/thrown away/found
2 fuss — bother/problem/idea
3 stunting ... growth — stopping physical development/retarding physical development/stimulating physical development
4 detrimental — harmful/very definite/uneven
5 thrive (on something) — exist/develop rapidly and positively/grow
6 embankments — fences to prevent crashing/emergency side lanes/the sloping banks at the side
7 soak ... up — absorb/eat/saturate
8 big deal — what a terrific result/astonishing/what does it matter
9 leaked out — flooded (out)/disappeared/passed through

Have you ever wondered what can be beneficial about radioactive waste dumped in the sea? Well, there's a four-foot lobster that's still growing off the coast of Cornwall who loves it. Why aren't we more grateful for the nuclear waste dumped in our environment? Consider what it's doing for the lobster, and imagine what it could do for your cabbages. It beats manure. You could even make a profit out of it — and the economy would really benefit.

There's always a silver lining behind the clouds of pollutant. Take the fuss people make about lead in petrol, for instance, stunting children's growth. That might have a grain of truth but doesn't automatically mean that it is detrimental to the environment. After all, exhaust fumes are full of nitrogen, and insects thrive on nitrogen — they can't get enough of it. They swarm on motorway embankments and soak it up. Small children get smaller and small insects get larger. Big deal.

Consider air-freshener. Said to freshen the furniture — kills your flowers. If it comes in an aerosol can, it'll help destroy the ozone layer too. Well, how useful is this ozone layer? I'm told there's a bald spot over the South Pole. It doesn't make any difference to me — I live in Bradford, though I do sometimes wonder how we'd cope if there really was a hole, and all the gravity leaked out. We'd all be living on our heads, or tied down to keep ourselves from drifting away, but everything else would be drifting around anyway.

3 Language

Conditional clauses

a Find all the conditionals in the text. Are they first or second? Identify the *if* clause relevant to the 'half' conditionals. Why is the *if* clause not given each time?

b It is often not necessary to provide the full two-clause conditional. Very often the missing 'half' is understood from the context. Listen and read these dialogues. What is the second 'half' to each of the conditionals?

1 A Imagine a world with four foot lobsters and five foot marrows.
B There'd be no shortage of food … and we'd be able to feed everyone. Each country would have it's own reactor …
A … and it's own instant manure to fertilise the fields …
B And everybody happy.
A If only …

2 C Go on, change your car to unleaded petrol.
D It'll cost me a fortune.
C Typical of so many people. What'll happen to the next generation?
D They'll probably develop immunity.

4 Speak

If you study the passage, it is possible to derive various conditionals. For example:

If children breathe lead-polluted air, their growth is stunted.

If flies breathe oxygen-rich air, they grow bigger.

How many conditionals can you make based on the passage? Use negative forms as well as positive. Vary the order of the clauses.

Section C

1 Speak

List four events/things that you think will happen as a result of our destruction of the environment. Note the reasons why.

Make a statement to the class giving your opinion and reasoning. Remember to change your language to reflect the degree of certainty you feel. Be prepared to defend your point of view if you are challenged.

2 Discuss

Think about the world today. Think of ten urgent actions the UN could take to prevent the destruction of the environment.

Exchange your views. Choose the best ten actions. Explain your choice to the class.

Learner Skills

- predicting content of text
- work on tone and reference in a text
- speculating on world issues
- exchanging and justifying opinions

Exam Skills

	Listening
A3b	comprehension of text
Exam	
	Reading
B1b	interpreting tone/style
	English in Use
B2	guessing meaning in context
	Speaking
C1	making statements with justification
	Speaking
C2	negotiating

EXAM SECTION

ENGLISH IN USE   Section A

Read the article below. Complete the text by circling the letter
next to the word which best fits each space from the list below.

Small, but Beautiful

Practical green ideas around the world will be
(1) _____ tomorrow when this year's Right
Livelihood Award — known as the Alternative Nobel
Prize — goes to a powerful Japanese housewives' co-
operative that promotes 'self-managed and less wasteful
(2) _____'.

The Award, presented in the Swedish parliament a day
before the (3) _____ Nobel Prize ceremony, will
also share out cash grants of $120,000 to Survival
International, which campaigns from London for tribal
victims of (4) _____ 'development', two
Ethiopian doctors who practise a village-based treatment
for Bilharzia; and an Ethiopian agronomist who has
found a way of saving seed species from destruction by
modern farming methods.

This is the tenth year of the award invented by Jakob
van Uexkull, half Swede, half German, who
(5) _____ the (6) _____ £500,000 by
selling his stamp business. He says he is not against the
Nobel Prize and offered that august body his services to
start a section for the environment, peace and the third
world. When they refused, he set up the alternative —
'to reward people with practical, exemplary, and

replicable solutions'.

This year's winner, the Seikatsu Club, began in 1965
when a Tokyo housewife organised 200 women to buy
cheaper milk.

Employing 700 people with a turnover of 41 billion yen,
the co-operative (7) _____ 400 products to
members, including rice, milk, chicken, eggs, fish and
vegetables and 60 original food brands. They believe
'housewives can begin to create a society that is harmo-
nious with nature by taking action from the home.

Other ideas include:

- The Lokayan group who (8) _____ local
  action in Indian villages, helping protect civil
  liberties, women's rights and the environment.

- Frances Moore-Lappe, author of *Diet for a Small
  Planet*, who argued that (9) _____ is caused
  more by bad 'development' than over-population or
  poverty.

- The Ladakh ecological development group, preserv-
  ing a traditional culture from the onslaught of
  tourism and (10) _____ development.

1	a revered	(b) honoured	c hounded	d celebrated
2	(a) lifestyles	b lives	c households	d companies
3	a repeated	(b) reputable	(c) regular	d reliable
4	(a) thoughtless	b helpless	c thoughtful	d thinking
5	a got	b acquired	c borrowed	(d) raised
6	(a) first	b developed	c third	d whole
7	(a) distributes	b advertises	c gives	d contributes
8	a co-operate	(b) co-ordinate	c control	d conceive
9	a erosion	(b) famine	c nourishment	d flooding
10	a rapid	b controlled	(c) unplanned	d unprepared

READING

Read the first part of this article on Black Holes.

For questions **1–5** you must choose which of the extracts **A–F** match the numbered gaps in the text. There is one additional extract which does not belong in any of the gaps.

A Both the theory of black holes and the evidence for their existence are products of 20th century science.

B Since such heavy stars should produce a lot of light, Laplace therefore concluded that the most brilliant of stars must be invisible.

C The debate is a fascinating one, particularly as it seems to indicate that much of science fiction could perhaps, after all, be science fact.

D Around the black hole itself, there is, too, another gaping hole, a few miles across, where space does not even exist.

E Black holes can turn the reality we know into chaos. They warp space and time and should lead us to greater understanding of the Universe.

F Subsequent measurement and experimentation have confirmed Einstein's theory; and with Einstein's view of the Universe, astronomers are now confident of being able to calculate their way around — and even into — a black hole.

Inside a

BLACK HOLE

BLACK HOLES CAN TURN EVERYTHING WE KNOW ABOUT REALITY ON ITS HEAD. INFINITELY DENSE, THEY WARP SPACE AND TIME, AND THEY MAY EVEN CONNECT DIRECTLY WITH OTHER UNIVERSES.

For years, scientists the world over have argued whether black holes are in fact a dead-end to nowhere or perhaps secret passages through space and time.

1 [gap]

But what exactly is a black hole? Quite literally, it is a gap in the fabric of space, torn from our Universe by a star collapsing in on itself. It is a region into which matter has fallen and from which nothing, not even light, can escape. Within the black hole, there is no up or down, no left or right; and time and space have changed roles.

Just as on Earth we cannot help but travel forward in time, so any space traveller unfortunate enough to fall into a black hole would be sucked into the centre by an infinite density and crushed out of existence.

2 [gap]

Here, the pull of gravity is stronger than anywhere else in the Universe, and nothing can ever escape from it.

What is more, even if we could fly into a black hole, we could never inform the rest of the Universe what lies within, since signals could never be relayed through this exceptional gravity.

However, the mathematics of gravity, based on Einstein's theory of relativity, can tell us much about the nature of these odd phenomena.

3 [gap]

But surprisingly, the first predictions of black holes were made in 1798 by the French astronomer Pierre Laplace. In his Exposition du Systeme du Monde, Laplace proposed the startling and seemingly contradictory theory that the most luminous stars might in fact be invisible.

INVISIBLE STARS

Laplace derived this theory from Newton's law of gravitation. If a star has the same density as the Earth, Laplace argued, it would be so massive that its surface gravity would prevent light from escaping.

4 [gap]

The modern view, however, is that stars as heavy as those described by Laplace cannot exist in reality. Indeed astronomers now think that black holes are formed not by the massive explosion predicted by Laplace but by a cataclysmic implosion — matter being dragged inwards and compressing to an incredible density.

The main source of contemporary theories about black holes was in fact Albert Einstein. In his General Theory of Relativity, published in 1916, Einstein replaced Newton's 'force' of gravity with an entirely new concept of time and space 'warps'.

5	

Using Einstein's equations, the German astronomer Karl Schwarzschild produced a general description of black holes only months after publication of the general theory.

ENGLISH IN USE Section B

Read the following notes which were taken in a geography lecture. Using the information given, complete the formal description of glaciers by writing the missing words in the spaces provided on the right. The first answer has been given as an example.

Use **not more than two words** in each space.

A glacier is a (1) … ice which moves (2) … down a valley from above the snowline under (3) … of gravity. It is (4) … owing to the (5) … of the immense (6) … of snow, which depresses the (7) … . The snow in the (8) … layers (9) … and then solidifies again into (10) … . Under the (11) … pressure this (12) … into clear ice.

(1)   **mass of**
(2) _____
(3) _____
(4) _____
(5) _____
(6) _____
(7) _____
(8) _____
(9) _____
(10) _____
(11) _____
(12) _____

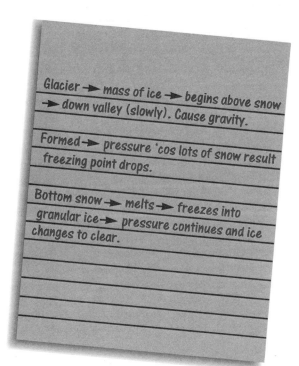

Glacier ➡ mass of ice ➡ begins above snow ➡ down valley (slowly). Cause gravity.

Formed ➡ pressure 'cos lots of snow result freezing point drops.

Bottom snow ➡ melts ➡ freezes into granular ice ➡ pressure continues and ice changes to clear.

THE THINGS WE DO

16

1 Vocabulary

List as many adjectives as you can similar in meaning to *weird* and as many nouns as you can similar in meaning to *a madman/woman*.

2 Speak

Look at the picture. Decide what you think this could be; what it might be used for; who it might be used by. Report your ideas to the class.

3 Language

Modal verbs for deduction/speculation

We use modals to express our certainty (or lack of it) about something.

In the affirmative we can use:

will, must, could, may, might, to have to

In the negative we use:

will not, cannot, could not, may not.

Which of these meanings is expressed by each of the following phrases?

certainty   possibility   doubt   impossibility

1   It could be a satellite.
2   It won't be ready yet.
3   It has to be a trick.
4   It can't be a microscope.
5   It may be a game.
6   It'll be a telescope.
7   It must be a new invention.
8   It couldn't be a toy.
9   It might be a measuring instrument.
10 It may not be a tool.

Pronunciation

a   Listen to these speakers and order them according to the degree of certainty expressed. Write the number in the box.

b   Listen to this one sentence: *It could be a solution* said in four different ways. What meaning is expressed each time? Write the number in the box.

	a	b
absolute certainty	☐	☐
possibility	☐	☐
doubt	☐	☐
absolute impossibility	☐	☐

4 Speak

Restate your thoughts about the object in the photograph. What is the likelihood of each person's suggestion being correct?

5 Read

a Skim the text and find out what the object was used for.

Ultrasonic gun 'nobbles' winning racehorse

Last year the racehorse Ile de Chypre was winning a race at Ascot. Suddenly a blast from an ultrasonic gun caused the horse to bolt and lose the race.

This ultrasonic gun disguised as a pair of binoculars was used to 'nobble' the leading horse at Royal Ascot, a court was told last week. James Laming created the weapon by reading the Encyclopaedia Britannica section on ultrasonics.

The device is very small and simple to conceal. A pair of binoculars is attached to a large leather case. Under the lens caps there are two high powered 'ceramic transducers' really a pair of very high powered loud speakers.

The weapon is powered by a pair of industrial cadmium batteries, concealed in the case, no larger than a packet of cigarettes. This gives the gun a range of 50 feet at its high power.

Ile de Chypre was three lengths clear last year in the King George V Handicap. The binoculars were pointed at the horse and James' brother, Robert, pulled the trigger. The horse heard a shrieking, terrifying noise, which no human could hear at all.

For the horse, the noise is best described as listening to very loud feedback from a microphone, or as Mr Laming described it: 'the horse feels like he has got a hornet or wasp in his ear'. The horse threw its jockey, Greville Starkey, to the ground as it veered sharply to the left and bolted.

After the race there was a stewards' enquiry into why the horse should suddenly have behaved as it did. No conclusions were drawn but there were many rumours that Greville Starkey might have deliberately thrown the race.

The jockey was always sure of his innocence, and blamed the incident on a flash from a camera. He claims he would have won the race by five or six lengths if the incident had not happened.

The accused, Mr Laming, left school at the age of 15. He educated himself through reading and had created a 'stun gun' based on bright light, which had been banned by the Home Office.

Exam **b** Read the article and find the correct answer to these questions.

1 If the incident had not happened, Ile de Chypre
   A could well have won the race.
   B would have won the race.
   C could not have won the race.

2 Nobody saw the device because
   A it was no larger than a packet of cigarettes.
   B it was very high-powered.
   C it looked like a leather case and a pair of binoculars.

3 The noise was so strong, the horse
   A fell to the ground.
   B was deafened.
   C actually felt pain.

4 The stewards' enquiry
   A decided that the jockey had lost the race deliberately.
   B did not manage to find the cause.
   C decided that the jockey was innocent.

5 The jockey thought
   A the horse had been frightened by a camera flash.
   B the horse had been blinded.
   C he was to blame for the incident.

6 The inventor of the device
   A had used a stun gun on a horse before.
   B had invented other devices before this one.
   C had invented another dangerous gun before this one.

Section B

1 Listen

Exam

Listen to these three descriptions of recent scientific advances and read the following information. Some mistakes were made when typing this sheet from notes. Look at numbers 1–10. If you think the information is correct, do nothing. If you think the information is wrong, make any correction necessary.

Recent Research

TRANSPLANTS

Reason:	1	lack of human organs to transplant
Research:	2	completed results next year
Aim:		to develop animal organs to transplant into humans
How:	3	by improving the genes in the organs

ONCOMOUSE

Reason:		to study cancer and other illnesses
Research:	4	already created a half dog half wolf, also the Oncomouse.
Facts on Oncomouse:	5	sometimes develops cancer after 90 days then is cured
How:	6	genetic engineering

NANOMACHINES

Reason:		to heal/cure/repair the world
Facts:		a miniscule machine size
	7	1 billionth of a mile
Uses:		in atmosphere
	8	to spread acid rain/repair the ozone layer
	9	in human brain to cure illness eg. reduce cholesterol
		in house to eg. eliminate dust
How:	10	by manipulating matter

2 Discuss

In groups, choose one of the inventions. Listen again, make notes. Discuss the following issues:

    the value to society
    the cost
    the moral/ethical point of view
    the feasibility
    the public attitude.

Report your findings/conclusions to the class.

Section C

1 Speak

a Consider each item in the photographs. Think of as many possible purposes for each; how they could each be used; what or who they could be used by; where and when they would be used; which the most useful is.

b Compare your ideas and decide:
which explanation is the most plausible,
which is the most imaginative,
which is the most ridiculous.

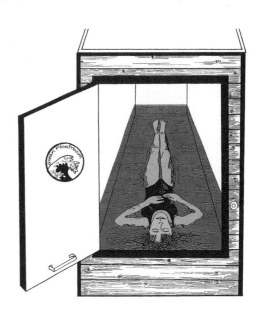

2 Listen

Exam

The inventions in the photos were all displayed at an exhibition entitled 'Life in the next century'. Listen to the announcements and complete the table.

	1	2	3
Name			
Purpose			
User			
Buyer			

3 Write

Exam

You attended the exhibition and you now have to write a report on it for a health/sports club. (150–200 words)

Step 1 Go over and consolidate the information you have. Listen again if necessary. Choose one of the items to focus on in detail.

Step 2 Decide what the effects of installing such an item would be. Add your recommendations to your notes.

Step 3 Organise your notes according to this plan: introduction — mention of variety of items — detailed description of chosen item — conclusion. Finalise the content of each paragraph.

Step 4 Write out the report. Consider the grammar, punctuation and spelling very carefully. If in doubt check before writing.

Step 5 Proof-read your report but make only minor error corrections. Be very neat and tidy with any corrections. Do not make major changes at this point.

Exam Strategies

During the exam, you do not have time to follow the procedure of notes — draft — proof-read — good copy. It is advisable therefore to: make notes — organise them — write — correct minor errors. From now on in this course the writing of draft copies is not advised.

4 Language

'Wh' clauses

a Look through the unit and note down all the examples of 'Wh' clauses that you find.

b Study the following examples. Tick the correct ones and correct the incorrect ones.
1 You have to say what do you think?
2 Tell us how can we win.
3 You don't know what it might be used.
4 He doesn't mind to where he gets.
5 Do you know when will she arrive?
6 Did you say who was this used by?
7 Who they see and who they speak to is their business.
8 You can't say how much might they lose, you don't know.

Cleft sentences

In 7 above the order of the clauses has been changed. This focuses attention on the content of the 'Wh' clause. In such cases the 'Wh' clause is the subject of the sentence and functions like a noun. We can rewrite 7 like this:
It is their business who they see and who they speak to.

a Some sentences re-arrange quite easily. Complete the following:
1 More time is what we need. What we need is …
2 Success is what you must work for. What …
3 Work hard was what he did. What …

b Others require the addition of a subject *it*. Complete the
following:

4 When you leave is up to you. It is up to you when …

5 How you get there is your problem. It is …

6 What she does is her choice. It …

7 It does not matter the number of times you try.
The number of times …

8 It does not matter what he said. What …

9 It was inexcusable what he did. What …

c We can use cleft sentences to emphasise almost any
information we choose. Consider this sentence:
My sister tried the float tank last week.

We can say:
It was my sister (who/that) tried the float tank last week.
– to stress *who*
It was last week (that) my sister tried the float tank.
– to stress *when*
It was a float tank (that) my sister tried last week.
– to stress *what*.
What my sister did was try the float tank last week.
– to stress *the action*.

Rewrite
Paul does not like the idea of genetic engineering.
to stress

1 what

2 the action

3 who

d Consider your feelings/reactions to some of the
ideas/inventions in this section. Make example sentences
with both constructions ('Wh' clauses and cleft sentences). Work with a partner to correct your work.
Discuss any problems with the teacher.

THE PARANORMAL

17

1 Read
Read the article and draw a rough sketch to show what it is about. Discuss the story and decide if you think it is true or not.

2 Vocabulary
List other paranormal phenomena which happen.

Then define or find out the definition for:

Poltergeists   Levitation
Clairvoyance   Ouija boards
Psychokinesis

Express the definitions in your own words.

3 Read
a Now read this newspaper article giving definitions for the above phenomena and see how similar yours are.

b Scan the text and list all the types of people involved in the paranormal.

Inga's Attraction!

Human magnet Inga Halduchenke stretched out her hand and from her palm dangled ... a collection of cooking pans, cutlery, pens and pencils.

The metal objects just stuck to the 12-year-old Ukranian school-girl. She told scientists: 'I have these magic powers, I don't know why'.

A scientist admitted: 'She was able to suspend objects weighing four kilos from the back of her hand. It was incredible.'

Some paranormal phenomena defined

POLTERGEISTS: They nearly always focus on children or teenagers, particularly. This is thought to be because at those ages the mind, like the body, is developing and at its most sensitive.
Poltergeists are noisy, mischievous ghosts that tend to throw objects around and generally create havoc. That they still seem to exist so widely makes them one of the most alarming psychic phenomena.

CLAIRVOYANCE: The ability to see things which are not ordinarily visible to the human eye. A clairvoyant can guess the sequence of cards in a shuffled pack and can read the contents of a sealed letter.

PSYCHOKINESIS: Possessors of this power are thought to be able to change or move objects just by concentrating on them. Uri Geller is probably the most famous, and disputed, possessor of this power.

LEVITATION: Some psychokinetics can make themselves, other people or objects rise several feet above the ground. This is called levitation.

OUIJA BOARDS: Ouija board participants place their fingers on the bottom of an upturned glass resting on the board. After a while the spirit communicator will move the glass towards certain letters of the alphabet which are displayed on the board.
When put together, the letters often spell out messages. Ouija is not always taken seriously and often the unconscious (or conscious) muscular actions of the participants move the spirit marker.

Section B

1 Read

Read this text to find out how levitation can occur.

In groups, try the ritual. Follow it very closely and see what happens. Discuss your results. Are there any explanations?

2 Listen

a Listen to one explanation put forward by a doctor who witnessed the teenagers' experiment. Do you agree or disagree with what she says?

b The editor of the newspaper was the second person they lifted. Listen to his report of his experience. Make notes and report what he said.

3 Read

What is the journalist's opinion of the explanation you just heard? As you read, fill in the blanks from this list:

will   could   might
been able to   could not

4 Listen

a What does the boy who was lifted say about the experiment?

Exam

b Listen to those who lifted the boy give their impression. Fill the blanks with the speaker's name: Carrie, Oliver, Zack, Lily, Cassie.

_____ describes the ease of the second lift.

_____ gives a reason for the difficulty first time.

_____ contrasts the first and second times.

_____ was astonished (for a while).

_____ gives reasons why it worked.

Four teenagers attempted to lift seven-and-a-half stone Anthony (seated) by their index and middle fingers. Needless to say, they found it extremely difficult. But then they performed a ritual which, they were told, would apparently help to decrease his weight. At first, many of them were sceptical.

Daisy Monahan put her right hand firmly on Anthony's head. She counted 'one'. The boy to her left did the same. He counted 'two'. The boy to his left did the same. He counted 'three'. This continued until all hands, both right and left, were resting on Anthony's head. Then, slowly, they started to count down again, taking their hands off the head as they did so. When the head was free of all hands, Daisy counted 'One, two, three lift'. They lifted. Anthony seemed to have lost several stone in only a handful of seconds. Some of the sceptics were gob-smacked.

Later on, four teenage boys tried to lift a 13-stone man by the same method. They couldn't lift him at all at first. But after the ritual, they lifted him two feet into the air.

How did this happen?

The Indy wasn't totally satisfied with Dr Robinson's theory. So we put together a weight of exactly a quarter of the initial 13-stone load.

We asked each boy to try and lift it individually. One of the larger boys (1) _____ lift it, but only after a great deal of strain. The others (2) _____ lift it at all. And yet they'd (3) _____ lift exactly that weight with ease, only seconds before, when they lifted a 13-stone man.

So what was happening? Dr Robinson wasn't sure. She suggested that it (4) _____ have something to do with the position of the person lifting.

Perhaps the explanation is as simple as that. But we at *The Indy* prefer to think that the true answer remains a mystery. If there is a conventional explanation for the phenomenon (as well there might be), we do not believe we have heard it yet. Any theories you want to send in, we (5)_____ put to the test.

5 Language

Expectations

a Listen again to Carrie. Write down her exact words after *But I expect … .*
What pattern follows *expect*? (Ignore the *if* clause)
Does *expect* in this sentence mean:
1 wait for   2 hope for   3 suppose

b Try to say Carrie's words in another way, still using *I expect … .*
What other patterns can follow *I expect …*?

c Say what your expectations would be:
  • if you were about to try this experiment.
  • if extra-terrestrials landed in your country tomorrow.
  • if your country won the next World Cup (Football).

Noun phrase with *of -ing*

a Dr Robinson used the following sentence:
The expectation of being lifted again will make the body more tense.

Underline the subject (noun phrase). What words can be substituted? Give examples.

b Rewrite the following sentences beginning each with an appropriate noun phrase.

1 He hoped to see the results and that excited him.
2 There was danger and she could be hurt but this was not one of her considerations.
3 They would have some fun and this prospect cheered her up.
4 Levitation was not an idea which appealed to me.
5 She is going to be in court and this will be useful experience for her.
6 He was afraid he would fail the exam and this stopped him studying.
7 He expected he would see a ghost and this thrilled him.

Reported Speech

Listen again to the teenagers' comments on the experiment. For each speaker write a report of what they said.

Section C

1 Speak

Have you ever had any experience at all of any paranormal phenomena? Or do you know of anyone else who has? Make notes and prepare a short talk describing one experience. Listen to each others' accounts and then discuss them.

2 Write

Exam

Write a letter to *The Indy* newspaper describing the experience you talked about (200–250 words).

Step 1 Think about the layout, addresses, date, endings, etc.

Step 2 Organise your notes on the story into a logical sequence and divide into paragraphs.

Step 3 Write the beginning and the introductory sentence, followed by an expansion of your notes. Finish with set phrases appropriate to the context.

Step 4 Proof-read for minor errors. Correct neatly.

Learner Skills

- understanding facts in texts
- defining words/explaining meaning
- giving opinion in response to text
- expressing expectations
- reporting what people said
- long turn speaking
- formal letter writing

Exam Skills

English in Use
B3 developing skill for gapfilling exercise

Listening
B4 matching speakers
Exam

Speaking
C1 confidence with long turn speaking

Writing
C2 formal letter writing
Exam

WHAT ON EARTH!

18

1 Discuss

a Look at these photographs. What do you call this type of being?

b What other movies about aliens can you think of? Discuss why you think these types of movies are popular. What age range/type of people do they appeal to? What do you think of them?

2 Language
Exclamations of shock/disbelief
What might an English speaking person say if an alien walked into their living room? Draw up a class list of possible exclamations.

Pronunciation
Which of these exclamations are on your list? Practise repeating/imitating the speakers on tape paying particular attention to the intonation.

Modals with conditionals
The following sentence expresses certainty.
If an alien walked into my room I'd scream.

Study the following variations. What does each of them express?
a If an alien walked into my room I doubt that I'd scream.
b If an alien walked into my room I might probably scream.
c If an alien walked into my room I could scream.
d If an alien walked into my room I suppose I might scream.
e If an alien walked into my room I'd never scream.

Pronunciation
Mark any words which would be stressed and practise saying them aloud.

3 Speak
Now consider your own reaction. What would/might you do? Give a suitable sentence for each degree of likelihood. Talk to others about their own reactions.

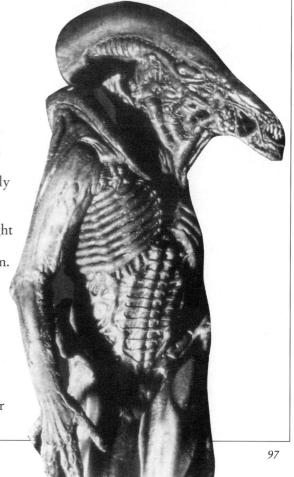

1 Read

What are 6,000 Americans frightened of?
What have they done about their fear?

What is the significance of the following verbs?
to flock   to launch   to snap up

Can you think of any other verbs which could
replace them?

> **SPACE FANS** are flocking to
> Mike St. Lawrence's firm — to
> buy £10 million insurance
> against being kidnapped by
> UFO-flying aliens. Mike, of
> Altamonte Springs, Florida,
> launched the policy as a joke. It
> has been snapped up by 6,000
> cash customers.

2 Read

The following article appeared in *The Guardian* newspaper on
10 October 1989. The incident was reported in other papers as
well.

a Skim read the article. What is your initial reaction to it?

b Fill in the blanks with suitable words. Only one word per
blank.

c Read the article and make two lists, one of definite, known
facts, the other of claims about the incident. Compare your
list with the class and discuss any discrepancies.

Underline the words or phrases which indicate lack of
certainty or doubt.

Russians 'sight alien beings'

SCIENTISTS in the Russian city of Voronezh say they have evidence (1) _____ back up eyewitness reports that an unidentified flying object recently landed in a park there.

According to the news agency Tass, local people saw a large shining disc hover (2) _____ the park and land. A hatch opened and out came 'one, two (3) _____ three creatures similar to humans, and also a small robot'.

'The aliens were three or even four metres (10–13 feet) tall, but with very small heads', the news agency quoted witnesses as saying. They walked round and then went (4)_____ again. Eyewitnesses were terrified for several days, Tass said.

Mr Genrikh Silanov, head of the Voronezh geophysical laboratory, told Tass he and his team have identified the exact spot.

'We detected a circle 20 metres (5) _____ diameter, plus four dents of about four to five centimetres in depth. We also found two mysterious pieces of rock.

'At first glance they looked like sandstone of a deep red colour. However mineralogical analysis has shown (6) _____ the substance cannot be found on Earth. But additional tests are needed to reach a more definite conclusion', he said.

The scientific findings of (7) _____ the UFO landed matched witnesses accounts, he said. The Tass story comes after a flood of stories about UFO's in (8)_____ Russian press.

Mr Anatoly Listratov, head of the department studying anomalous phenomena at the All-Union Geodescial Society, last week reported a sighting by two pilots.

One was blinded after seeing a strange object, and the other later died of cancer.

He said the causes of UFO's were still unknown, (9) _____ because Russian scientists refuse to study them properly or publish their results.

Officers working on missile and space projects (10) _____ reported numerous sightings.

3 Vocabulary

a What is the difference between *sighting* and *sight*? What is the difference between *to be blind* and *to be blinded*?

b What do the following words mean in the text:

a hatch
a a sort of door   **b** window   **c** stair

to back up
a to prove   **b** to support   **c** to confirm

witness
a person **a** who knows something   **b** who sees something   **c** who discovers something

findings
a results   **b** discoveries   **c** research

UFO
a unknown foreign object   **b** unknown flying observer   **c** unidentified flying object

c Select four of the words/phrases you do not know. Use reference books and find out the meaning within this context. Explain them to the class.

4 Role play

Work in groups of three. One of you is Mr Silanov — consider what questions to ask the local people.

The other two are local eyewitnesses — think what happened to you. Discuss this and agree on some facts.

Role play the meeting and the interview which followed.

Learner Skills

- speculating on unreal situations
- expressing shock/disbelief

Exam Skills

English in Use
B2b   gap filling exercise
Exam

EXAM SECTION

Read this newspaper article. The text is followed by a number of unfinished statements about the text. You must choose the answer which you think fits best.

Experts from Japan, Canada and the States have been swarming over our fields examining the circles.

The Sun has investigated the different theories and asked the experts what they think.

1 Mini-cyclones: Dr Terence Meaden, of the Tornado and Storm Research Organisation, believes they are caused by whirlwinds. But Professor Archibald Roy, of Glasgow University's Astronomy Department says 'They (1) _____'

2 UFOs: Circle expert Colin Andrews believes the rings could be messages from another life form. He says: 'Lights have been seen hovering above the ground where circles are later discovered'.

3 Helicopter: Some believe they are caused by choppers. But an Army spokesman says: 'A helicopter could only make that shape if it was flying upside down over the same spot — then it would crash!'

4 Wildlife: Theories include demented hedgehogs running in circles. But experts say it would take 40,000 hedgehogs to make one small circle.

5 Pranksters: Some claim the circles are an elaborate hoax. But scientists say (2) _____ rule this out.

6 Ghostly presence: Many circles appear above archaeological sites. Ghost Club chairman Tom Perrot says: 'They could be caused by paranormal forces'.

7 Hailstones: The Met Office has refuted the giant hailstone theory, arguing that 'ice bombs' would by now (3) _____ causing massive damage.

8 Ozone layer: Holes in the ozone layer could allow through ultra-violet rays which could cause crops to collapse. But an environmentalist says: 'This doesn't explain the perfect symmetry'.

9 Fungus: Some experts claim that fungus could cause the pattern. But plant pathologist David Lockley says: 'The circles look (4) _____ by fungus.'

10 Soil disorder: It is said a chemical imbalance in chalky soils could affect the crop. But a Ministry of Agriculture expert says: 'Soil disorders (5) _____.'

A wouldn't form perfect circles
B could not have been made naturally
C have been thought to be
D the number and size of the circles
E too regular to have been formed
F have struck a major city

Exam Strategies

Gapped text (sentence or phrase) — English in Use. To complete the text, select the correct pieces from the list of possibilities. About 5 blanks to 8 options. Procedure: skim read the text. Read more carefully to the first blank. Think what the author is saying. Read what follows the blank. Then select from the options available. Try out every option in the gap. If a full stop is shown you can ignore the options which cannot be complete sentences. Do not waste time if you do not get the answer immediately. Read on following the same procedure. Work steadily through the text, going backwards and forwards to check. Remember: always think what the author is saying; read what follows just as much as what precedes; check every entry several times.

SPEAKING   Phase B

Choose one of the pictures below and describe it to your partner (who has the same six pictures). At the end of one minute your partner must say which picture you were describing.

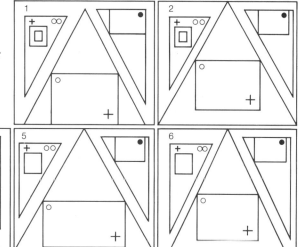

ENGLISH IN USE   Section B

In most lines of the following text there is a word missing. Read the text and put a slash (/) where the word should go and write the word in the space provided at the end of the line. Some lines are correct. Indicate these with a tick (✓) against the line number. The first two lines have been done as examples.

The Phantom Face

1	Poltergeists / seems, sometimes haunt commercial premises	1	*it*
2	as well / invading the home. In 1973, Manfred Cassirer	2	*as*
3	a member of the council Britain's Society for Psychical	3	
4	Research — was called in to investigate an odd series of	4	
5	events that had occurred a garden centre occupying two rough	5	
6	sheds in Bromley, Kent. Planks of wood often mysteriously	6	
7	vanished, only to reappear out of the blue. A clock seen	7	
8	to jump off a desk, apparently of own accord. Then, worst	8	
9	of, garden fertilizer started falling from the ceiling, even	9	
10	it was not stored at that height. On one occasion, it even	10	
11	formed the shape of a face, modelled in two distinct of	11	
12	fertilizer (grey and white), on a counter. Stranger still,	12	
13	the skull-like shape remained static when looked at, but	13	
14	disintegrate somewhat whenever Cassirer looked. Finally,	14	
15	after Cassirer had investigated on two occasions, it	15	
16	disappeared just mysteriously as it had arrived.	16	

FATE

1 Read

a Study these dictionary entries and think about the definitions. Are there any differences? Are there any similarities?

b Does everything that happens in life have meaning? Is it controlled or accidental? Do individuals have control over their own lives?

chance /tʃɑːns/ noun **1** [c.] an opportunity: *I didn't have a chance to thank you yesterday. This job is the chance of a lifetime.* **2** [c.] a risk; a possibility that something bad will happen: *Don't take any chances.* **3** [c or u.] the possibility or likelihood of being successful: *There's a good chance that she'll get the job.* **4** [u., also adj. a.] something that happens because of luck etc and is not expected or planned: *a chance discovery. I only found out by chance.*

2 Vocabulary

You often hear the following expressions:

By chance
A lucky coincidence
To happen to do something
What a coincidence!
What luck to ...
A chance encounter
Chance would be a fine thing
The luck of the draw

Find out the meaning of each. Write an example and provide an explanatory situation for each.

fate /feɪt/ noun **1** [u.] the power that is believed by some people to control events and that is impossible to influence. **2** [c.] what has happened or will happen to a person: *My fate was to be born short and fat.* **3** [c.] (often *the — of sb,st*) the future (of somebody or something): *What will be the fate of the world if the ozone layer is destroyed?*

coincidence /kəʊˈɪnsədəns/ noun c. or u (an example of) the surprising fact of two or more things being the same or happening at the same time as if you had organized it: *What a coincidence; you're just the person I need to see!* co‚inciˈdental adj. co‚inciˈdentally adv.

Section B

1 Read

Here is an account of the survival of two young children. Read the article and make a list of all the people involved. Underline any examples of the words and phrases in A2, above. Read a second time and list all the coincidences that occurred.

2 Language

Third conditional

Referring to the text, complete this sentence with as many different clauses as you can:
The children would have died if …

Both clauses refer to the past. No changes are possible so all we can do is speculate how the world would have been different if … What other possible words could be substituted for *would* in the first clause? Compare your choices and decide if the meaning is changed in any way. Look at the sentences you wrote above. Could you have substituted any other word for *would* in any of them?

3 Vocabulary

Underline the words in the left-hand column in the text. Then answer the questions.

Babies in fjord live with luck after crash

Oslo: Two infants survived for 15 minutes under water inside a car which crashed into a Norwegian fjord
5 because of a series of lucky coincidences.
A car driven by their mother skidded on an icy road at the weekend and
10 crashed into the Gandsfjord, at Sandnes on Norway's west coast, police said yesterday.
The woman scrambled out
15 of the car but the infants, a four-month-old girl and a two-year-old boy, were trapped 30 feet under the surface of the near-freezing
20 water.
The first stroke of luck was that the driver of the first car flagged down by the woman was a local authori-ty worker with a radio link
25 to the fire brigade. The fire brigade employee who received the message knew the local diving club's base was near the scene of the
30 accident.
Their three divers, fully dressed for rescue work were found at the club, and reached the crashed car
35 within three or four min-utes. A doctor who hap-pened to be driving past when the divers brought the children to the surface
40 resuscitated them. Police said the two infants hearts had stopped beating when they were rescued after 15 minutes under water, but
45 both were expected to be discharged soon from hospi-tal.

skidded (line 8)	Under what conditions can a car skid? Can we substitute swerve in this sentence? Why/why not?
scrambled (line 13)	Was it easy or difficult for the woman to get out? Think of two other situations using this verb.
flagged down (line 23)	Which of these words could be substituted here? *stopped waved at hitched* Show what this word really means.
resuscitated (line 41)	Which of these words could be substituted? *saved brought back to consciousness awoken*
be discharged (line 46)	Which of these words could be substituted? *be sent home be sent away be allowed to leave*

Section C

1 Discuss

In pairs — A look at text 1 on page 168. B look at text 2 on page 173. Read your text and identify all the coincidences. Tell your partner about the coincidences in your text. Is there anything similar about them?

Have you ever heard about anything similar? Has your partner?

2 Read

Read the first part of the continuation of the article and fill in the blanks with items from this list:

> *during   both   neither*
> *not only   and yet*

3 Write

Exam

Look at the remainder of the article and at the sketches. Each sketch represents a further coincidence. Use this information to complete numbers 2 to 5.

The Diaries of Dorothy and Bridget

Again (1)_____ Dorothy and Bridget were separated when they were just a few weeks old, put up for adoption. They were not reunited until they were 34. (2)_____ that time (3)_____ knew they were a twin (4)_____ in 1960, and for that year only, when they were girls of 15, they both kept diaries. (5)_____ were they the same make and colour, but the days that had been filled out correspond exactly. Here are some other coincidences.

1 Dorothy called her son Richard Andrew, Bridget called hers Andrew Richard. Dorothy's daughter was called Catherine Louise, Bridget's Karen Louise. (It was going to be Catherine, but she changed it to please a relative.)
2 Both ..... Tiger.
3 Both ..... bedroom door ..... at night.
4 Both ..... piano to grade ..... stopped.
5 Both ..... when talking if they ..... nervous.

1 Listen

Two people talk about something 'strange' that happened in their lives. For each:
note what the stroke of fate/coincidence was.
say if each event was fate or coincidence.

2 Language
Conditional variations

Each person uses an unusual form of a third conditional, a different way of expressing the *if* condition.

a Listen carefully for the conditions and make a note of the patterns. The first speaker gives condition and result. What are they? The second speaker gives two conditions and one result. What are they?

b Rewrite each conditional using the *if* construction. Now rewrite each using the alternative forms.

c Think of coincidence and fate in your own life. Using all the possible third conditional patterns, write examples based on your life.

3 Speak

Think of your own life. There must be at least one occasion when you felt chance or coincidence played a part, such as bumping into someone from home when you were in a foreign country. Think about one such incident and make notes.

Tell others what might have happened in your life if … .
Comment on each others' experiences. Think carefully about pronunciation and meaning.

Learner Skills

- analysing implications in a text
- discussing and comparing experiences
- telling stories

Exam Skills

C2	*English in Use* skills for gapfilling exercise
C3 Exam	*English in Use* completing text from information
D1	*Listening* detailed listening
D3	*Speaking* developing confidence in long turn speaking

HISTORY

20

1 Discuss

What does this quotation mean?
Is it true? Comment and discuss.

This verse is commonly taught
to school children when learning
about the 15th Century
explorers.

Did Columbus really discover
America? What do you think?

"History is written by the Victors"

"In 1492 Columbus sailed the ocean blue"

2 Read

This is an entry from an encyclopaedia. It describes the original
inhabitants of the Americas.

a Read and make three lists: people, animals and food. It does
not matter if you do not understand exactly what a word
means as long as you can identify the category.

Amerindians, the indigenous peoples of North
and South America. They are usually classified as
a major branch of the Mongoloid peoples but are
sometimes described as a distinct racial group.
With the Inuits and Aleuts (who are unquestion-
ably Mongoloids), they were the inhabitants of
the New World at the time of the first European
exploration in the late 15th century. Their fore-
bears came from north-eastern Asia, most probably taking advantage of low sea levels during the
last Ice Age to cross the Bering Strait on land.
The earliest certain evidence suggests that people
were in America by 15,000 years ago but an earlier date seems increasingly likely. Recent controversial archaeological finds in Mexico, Chile,
Brazil, and elsewhere suggest a human presence
as early as 30,000 or more years ago. There could
have been several separate colonizations; the
Inuits and Aleuts are the descendants of the most
recent one, within the past 10,000 years. The first
colonizers brought little with them other than
simple stone tools and perhaps domesticated
dogs for hunting. As hunters and gatherers they
spread quickly south. There was plentiful game
to hunt using fine stone projectile points such as
those of the Clovis tradition.

The cultural development of Amerindians provides an interesting comparison with the Old
World. Agriculture, which started developing
7000 or more years ago, was based on maize,
squash, and beans, with manioc being grown in
tropical forest regions. With no suitable animals
to domesticate, apart from the llama and the
guinea-pig, and no draught animals to pull the
plough, the development of more mixed farming
was gradual. In the Andes, an advanced metal-
lurgical technology developed from 1000 BC.
Complex societies developed in many areas,
which grew into sophisticated civilizations, for
example, the Aztecs and Incas, but most collapsed after the arrival of the conquistadors and
other European explorers in the 16th century.

Exam **b** Read these statements and then re-read the text marking the statements True or False.

1 The Americas have been populated for at least 10,000 years.
2 The indigenous peoples were not mongoloids.
3 The original inhabitants crossed the sea to reach America.
4 Traces of very ancient inhabitants have been found in several countries.
5 Archaeologists agree that people were there 30,000 years ago.
6 The very early inhabitants had trouble finding food.
7 The very early inhabitants lived in agricultural communities.
8 They used a wide range of animals for many years.
9 Some societies developed great skill in metal work.
10 The arrival of Europeans signalled the end for their civilisations.

3 Discuss

How much do you know about what happened to the indigenous peoples following the arrival of European explorers? Exchange information in groups and make notes.
One person from each group gives the class a report of the discussion.

4 Listen

Exam
Here is an account of the colonisation of the North American Continent. The accompanying Information Sheet contains several errors. As you listen make any changes that are necessary so that the Information Sheet is correct.

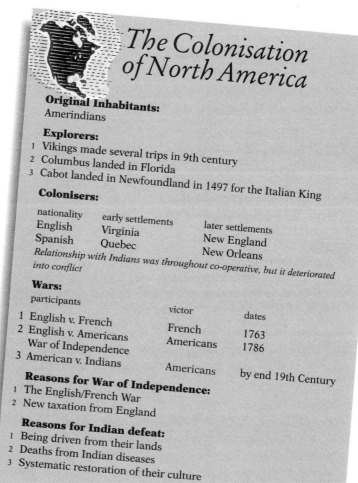

The Colonisation of North America

Original Inhabitants:
Amerindians

Explorers:
1 Vikings made several trips in 9th century
2 Columbus landed in Florida
3 Cabot landed in Newfoundland in 1497 for the Italian King

Colonisers:

nationality	early settlements	later settlements
English	Virginia	New England
Spanish	Quebec	New Orleans

Relationship with Indians was throughout co-operative, but it deteriorated into conflict

Wars:

participants	victor	dates
1 English v. French	French	1763
2 English v. Americans War of Independence	Americans	1786
3 American v. Indians	Americans	by end 19th Century

Reasons for War of Independence:
1 The English/French War
2 New taxation from England

Reasons for Indian defeat:
1 Being driven from their lands
2 Deaths from Indian diseases
3 Systematic restoration of their culture

Section B

1 Language
Mixed conditionals

a Which of the items in B can be used to correctly complete A?

A If the Red Indians had repulsed the colonising invaders ...

B ... they may not be oppressed any more.
... they'd have retained control of the North American continent.
... Europe would be crowded today.
... we will be more appreciative of their culture.
... Reagan would never have been president.
... the USA would not have the power that it does.

b Look at the correct results. Which of them are past results? Which of them are present results? Which of them are examples of the third Conditional? The remainder are mixed conditionals: past condition with present result. Both third and mixed conditionals are impossible and are purely speculative.

c Study the mixed conditionals. What grammatical forms are used:
    1 in the condition clause?
    2 in the result clause?

Complete the following conditionals with suitable clauses to make mixed conditionals.

1 If Hitler had never been born ...
2 If plastic had never been invented ...
3 If they had discovered life forms on the moon ...
4 ... private cars would not be polluting the air.
5 ... I would be very happy.
6 ... the UK would have a hotter climate.

2 Speak
Consider the following:
    If the North American Indians had prevented the colonisation movement in the 16th Century how might the world have been or be different?

Organise your speculations/conclusions according to whether the resulting change is in the past or in the present. Discuss your main speculations with the class.

3 Listen
Listen to this group of people discussing exactly the same subject. Note any results which are similar to your speculations.

Listen again and list all the results they mention. Identify which are past and which are present results.

4 Language
Conditionals in general

The subject for discussion above is a complete (third and mixed) conditional sentence containing two clauses. However as with first and second conditionals in conversation we frequently only state one of the clauses. We do this when either the condition or the result is known or is easily understood by all involved.

Listen again to the discussion and note when a complete two clause conditional is used. Note also how many results are given. Compare the two.

Introducing a hypothesis

In the discussion the speakers introduce their hypotheses with a variety of expressions.

I wonder if ...   I think ...
I suppose ...   Perhaps ...
Probably ...   I wonder now if perhaps ...

Listen again and tick the expressions as you hear them. Copy the way they say them.

Asking for confirmation

We often use question tags (*... isn't it? ... could he?*
... was she?) when we believe that something is true but we want confirmation from another person. Listen to these excerpts from the tape. Identify the tag in each.

Pronunciation

In the excerpts, do you think the intonation on the tag rises or falls? Practise saying the following. Remember you believe you are correct.

> *That's true, isn't it?*
> *You are going, aren't you?*
> *She is clever, isn't she?*

Write five other examples and practise saying them.

Section C

1 Task

Work in groups.

Step 1   Select another event in history. Prepare a short talk outlining what actually happened (according to what you know).

Step 2   Now introduce a hypothesis and see how many resulting changes you can think of.

Step 3   Organise these results into a logical order. Consider the degree of possibility and choose appropriate language to express each.

Step 4   Appoint two spokespersons, one to give the historical outline and the other to talk about the speculations. Give your talks to the class. At the end comment and speculate further.

2 Write

Write a short essay discussing your hypothesis (200–250 words). Include a description of the historical background, an introduction to the hypothesis, speculations on the results and conclusions.

Exam Strategies

From this point onwards, writing work designed for the writing exam will be presented as in the exam. There will be no more steps indicating procedure. It is suggested that you follow certain principles:

- make notes under organisational headings
- careful ordering/ organisation
- proof read

Learner Skills

- analysing and discussing meaning
- exchanging information
- speculating on the impossible
- intensive listening for content and language
- ways of introducing a hypothesis
- asking for confirmation

Exam Skills

	Reading
A2b	true/false statements
Exam	
	Speaking
A3	reporting on discussion
	Writing
C2	discursive essay writing
Exam	

ANECDOTE 21

1 Raiders, 70, in an **old-up!**

2 Thief roars off in Porsche

3 Moulting Girl

4 Dog leaves his owner **pegless!**

1 Discuss

Look at these headlines. What could they mean?
Make notes on each article — who it is about,
what possibly happened.

2 Read

a Match the articles to their headlines.

A A Chinese teenager is confounding doctors in Sichuan province by moulting after biting a python to death. Lian Lian was embraced by the serpent while she slept after bathing in a river.

After wrestling for two hours with the snake, which had a diameter 'bigger than a bowl of rice', Lian Lian took a huge bite out its neck and the python expired. Lian Lian was admitted to hospital with bruised legs, but four days later, doctors reported that she moulted 'from the chest to the feet' - a 'bizarre phenomenon' that continued for 3 months.

B A conman asked to test drive a £35,000 Porsche car - then roared off in it leaving the owner stranded in the road.

The thief had answered an advert in a local newspaper offering the Porsche 911 for sale.

The owner took him for a spin at Haywards Heath, Sussex, then got out to let the would-be buyer drive.

But before he could get back into the passenger seat, the high-performance car sped away.

C   A geriatric Bonnie and Clyde who rob fellow pensioners were being hunted last night.

The couple, in their 70s, snatched a purse with £23 and another containing £78 in daylight raids in ten minutes in shops in Old Swan, Liverpool.

In both cases, the tweed-clad woman chatted up their victims while her 'gentleman' lifted the loot.

They are thought to have fled by bus.

D An elderly dog-lover toppled over when he awoke from a nap.

For his 16-stone monster mongrel had chewed through his wooden leg.

The horrified pensioner crawled towards the dog, which was still munching on the false timber.

But the playful pooch - called Captain Pugwash - wouldn't give up his new toy.

Drugged

In desperation, the pegless pensioner phoned the RSPCA and the police.

But they could only get into the second-floor flat in London by pushing drugged meat through the letterbox.

Now Pugwash has been found a new home with computer manager Joanne de Nobriga in Bracknell, Berks — and his former owner has been fitted with a new leg.

Joanne, 32, said: 'The dog had obviously finished his food and was feeling a bit bored and playful.

'When the poor man woke up he had lost his leg. It's lucky that the dog picked on the wooden one!'

Exam **b** Read the articles and choose the correct alternative to the following:

1 Lian
  A loves snakes.
  B cuddled a python.
  C was squeezed by a python.

2 Lian
  A lost all her hair.
  B lost all her body hair.
  C went bald.

3 The thief
  A pretended to be a buyer.
  B wanted to test drive the car.
  C had always wanted a Porsche.

4 The dog owner was
  A old and retired.
  B a sea captain.
  C unemployed.

5 The dog
  A was dangerous.
  B attacked his owner.
  C wanted to play.

6 The pensioners stole
  A from shoppers.
  B from other old people.
  C from shops.

3 Vocabulary

a Find these words in each of the texts.

Text A python huge bruised bizarre phenomenon
Text B conman spin would-be
Text C geriatric pensioners raids tweed-clad the loot
Text D dog-lover nap mongrel timber pooch

Identify which are adjectives and which are nouns.

b Match each of the adjectives and each of the nouns to the definitions (of meaning in this context) given below.

Adjective definitions
• dressed in a particular type of material (Scottish) • strange • very old • wishing to be • very very large • with black and purple marks on the body

Noun definitions
• one who tricks people for financial gain • people over 60 years old • an attack to take money • a dog of mixed breed • stolen property • a remarkable or unusual 'thing' • wood • a short sleep • a ride • a type of very large snake • a slang word (dog) • someone who likes dogs

c Find the following expressions in the car thief article and write the infinitive pattern.
1 leaving the owner stranded
2 took him for a spin
3 let the would-be buyer drive
In your own words, say what each expression means in this context. Compare your definition with a partner.

d Find the phrasal verbs which mean the following. Give the infinitive pattern.
1 to talk to someone in order to become friendly
2 to drive away very quickly and noisily
3 to allow someone to take something
4 to fall down
Write your own example sentences using each phrasal verb.

e What words collocate with the following? Look in the articles if you cannot remember.
1 _____ a bag/purse (meaning to take)
2 _____ phenomena (strange)
3 _____ the loot (to steal)
4 _____ car (very fast)
5 _____ raid (during the daytime)

Think of other nouns which could collocate with the verbs/adjectives.

4 Role play

Work in pairs/threes. Choose one of the anecdotes, and read it again carefully. Imagine the conversation. Take the roles appropriate to your article and act out the scene.

1 Lian and the doctor/s when they first treated her.

2 The thief and the owner in the car up to the point of the theft.

3 The old couple and one of their victims.

4 The phone conversation between the pensioner and the police and/or the RSPCA.

1 Language

Verb tenses in the past

When you tell an anecdote, you begin by setting the scene.
The verb forms you use are very important.

Here are the beginnings of three anecdotes with the verbs
blanked out. Complete the texts by selecting a suitable verb
from the list and putting it in the correct form.
You may use the verbs as many times as you wish.

to be   to live   to work
to take   to lose   to happen
to drive   to go   to concern
to have

a I _____ on holiday in what _____ now Namibia and I _____ with some friends
along this road. Namibia _____ a very desolate country and you _____ for hundreds
of miles along straight roads and I _____ along …

b When I _____ a boy we _____ in Islington which _____ quite a run-down area in
those days and my mother _____ my younger brother and I to the market when we
_____ about 4 and 3 and she always _____ us. The first time this _____ she …

c This _____ a frightening experience I _____ when I _____ about 15 _____ in
an after-school job as a cleaner in a furniture factory and in this big factory everyone _____
it _____ quite empty…

2 Discuss

Imagine what each anecdote is about. Exchange your ideas.

3 Listen

a Now listen to the beginning of the first story and note any
differences in form. Discuss with the teacher if any alternatives are grammatically correct, appropriate and as meaning-
ful as the originals. Change any that are incorrect.

b Now listen to the complete anecdote. Work with a partner
and summarise what happened to Jeremy in one or two sentences. Compare your summary with others in the class.
Together, work out the best.

c Now do exactly the same with anecdotes b and c.

4 Language

Text organisation

a In telling an anecdote or story we:

1 give background information
2 describe the scene
3 recount the events/actions

Usually with one piece of information per block of text. Look
at the transcript on page 170 which shows these divisions.
Identify whether each is 1, 2 or 3. An example is given.

b Look at the transcript of b and c. Analyse the information
contained in the blocks of text.

c Note the verb tenses used in each category. Say also if the
verbs are state or event.

d Are the events in the stories told in chronological order?

Section   C

1 Task

Think of an anecdote, either something that happened to you or someone you know. Make notes thinking about the categories of information in B4 above. Set the scene, give the facts in a logical order, keep the surprise till the end. Practise telling your story. Remember to use short blocks. Now tell your anecdote to your group and listen to theirs.

2 Write

Write your anecdote as an article for a student newspaper (200 250 words). Remember that these types of anecdote are often presented as amusing (despite their often horrific side).

Give your article an appropriate heading.

Learner Skills

- predicting text content
- work on collocation
- analysing text organisation of information
- telling stories
- writing stories

Exam Skills

	Reading
A2b	vocabulary multiple choice
Exam	
	English in Use
B1	completing text
	Writing
C2	writing an article
Exam	

EXAM SECTION

READING

Read the following book reviews and answer questions 1–16.

A   **Margaret Forster** has taken an unusual line in her award-winning biography of the poet Elizabeth Barrett Browning. *Lady's Maid* (Chatto & Windus, £13.95) is a fictional account of the marriage of Elizabeth and Robert Browning, seen through the eyes of Lily Wilson, Elizabeth's maid.

Wilson's devotion is a double-edged sword, because she became trapped by the dependence of her mistress. 'You will not be able to leave her', warns a friend, 'you must not get pulled in too far.' Wilson, playing a supporting role in one of the most romantic Victorian love affairs, longs for a romance of her own. Forster's fictional approach gives her portrait of Barrett an extraordinary depth and immediacy, but Wilson is the real star of the story struggling to define herself within the dynamics of mistress and servant.

B   An imaginative, eccentric modern writer takes on a Victorian colossus, and the consequence is a major literary event that should keep bookish dinner parties arguing for months. **Peter Ackroyd's** gargantuan, thousand-page biography *Dickens* (Sinclair-Stevenson, £19.95) brilliantly delves into the genius of one of the greatest ever English novelists, exploring his tangled sexuality, and recreating the sights and smells of London in the 19th century. Ackroyd's Dickens is a man who is on the brink of madness: a workaholic, driven by a desperate, self-destructive energy; a mass of contradictions. Why did this arch-moralist, who extolled the virtues of hearth and home in his fiction, banish his middle-aged wife when she was worn out from child-bearing, and become hopelessly infatuated with a beautiful young actress half his age? Ackroyd combines fantasy with fact to arrive at the answers, and this is bound to cause a flurry of controversy among the purists.

C   Writing novels is all about telling stories — a hoary old cliché, perhaps, but worth repeating, especially when considering **Maeve Binchy.** Her best-selling stories of Irish life have an irresistible warmth and humour. *Circle of Friends* (Century, £13.99) follows a group of young Dubliners through University in the Fifties. There's fat, sweet Benny, her best friend Eve Malone, who was brought up by the nuns, and beautiful Nan, determined to snaffle herself a rich husband. This is just the book for a mellow autumn afternoon — as gripping as a rude blockbuster, but infinitely gentler and wiser.

D   American writer **Sara Paretsky** is the hottest name in crime fiction — her novels are far, far more than detective stories. *Burn Marks* (Chatto & Windus, £12.95) describes private-eye Victoria Warshawski's hard-fought battle to expose corruption among Chicago's political elite. Her popularity nose-dives when she starts to fit all the pieces together. An awful lot of people want to see her dead. Tough and pacey, yes, but it's also subtle, witty and realistic. Paretsky's feminist viewpoint sweeps away the clichés and tells it like it is.

E   *The Chatto Book of Love Poetry* (Chatto & Windus, £13.95) is the perfect gift for lovers — it features every aspect of romance, as described by writers down the centuries, from Chaucer to Ira Gershwin. Its editor, the poet **John Fuller**, has chosen to ignore historical order and placed ancient and modern verses side by side, to heighten the emotional impact. Whether you prefer the sweet simplicity of Leigh Hunt's *Jenny Kissed Me*, or the sheer voluptuous sensuality of Tennyson's *Now Sleeps the Crimson Petal*, you'll find something here to suit your mood.

Questions 1–5 ask about the type of book.

Books **1** _____ **2** _____ are fiction.

Book **3** _____ is non-fiction.

Books **4** _____ and **5** _____ are a mixture of fact and fiction.

The following questions refer to the description of the books in the review. When a question asks for more than one answer you may give the answers in any order. Some of the books will be mentioned more than once.

A Lady's Maid
B Dickens
C Circle of Friends
D Burn Marks
E The Chatto Book of Love Poetry

6 _____ and **7** _____ are deep and thought provoking.

8 _____ is controversial.

9 _____ and **10** _____ are sensitive and emotional.

11 _____ and **12** _____ are hard.

13 _____ and **14** _____ are romantic.

15 _____ and **16** _____ are humorous.

LISTENING Section D

You will hear various people talking about favourite movies. You will hear the series twice.

Task One Letters **A-H** list the type of movies. Put them in the order in which you hear them by completing the boxes numbered **1-8** with the appropriate letter.

Task Two Letters **I-P** list the reason why the speaker liked that particular film. Put them in order by completing the boxes numbered **9-16** with the appropriate letter.

Task One

A documentary	1	
B romantic	2	
C adventure	3	
D comedy	4	
E historical drama	5	
F horror	6	
G western	7	
H drama	8	

Task Two

I direction	9	
J good acting	10	
K excitement	11	
L the story	12	
M imagination	13	
N emotions provoked	14	
O suspense	15	
P blood and guts	16	

ENGLISH IN USE Section C

Choose the best phrase or sentence (given below the text) to fill each
of the blanks in the following text. Write one letter (**A–I**) in each of
the numbered spaces. Two of the suggested answers do not fit at all.

Maps of the Great Discoveries

At the beginning of their African voyages, the Portuguese pilots followed the same method of naviga-
tion as the seafaring peoples of the Mediterranean. From the marine charts (1) _____ and also its
distance. With the help of the mariner's compass and primitive methods of determining the vessel's
speed, (2) _____ estimating their position daily. In the Mediterranean, voyages were largely but
not exclusively a matter of coastwise sailing, (3) _____ and on the ability to recognise prominent
coastal landmarks, a high headland, a group of small islands, or a distinctively shaped mountain.
(4) _____ therefore rarely troubled to determine their latitude, partly also because the longitudinal
rangewas relatively small, and the degree of accuracy of their observations was not high.

When the Portuguese set out upon the waters of the Atlantic and made their way southwards along
the African coasts, they encountered different conditions. (5) _____ familiar landmarks were lacking on the coasts, which were often characterless for considerable stretches and a hostile local popula-
tion discouraged landings, (6) _____ They were also ranging through many degrees of latitude.
Inthese circumstances the pilots learned to determine the latitude by observing the altitude of the Pole
Star. As they progressed southwards (7) _____. These observations were made with the astrolabe
and with the quadrant.

A there was no body of sailors' knowledge to
draw on as regards winds and currents

B they tried to keep as close as possible to this
track

C its calculation at sea was extremely difficult

D pilots in the Mediterranean

E added to these was the possibility of being
blown off course into the ocean

F they worked out the direction of the
proposed voyage

G since the Pole Star does not coincide with the
celestial pole a correction was necessary

H they used the altitude of the sun combined
with mathematical tables

I so that much reliance was also placed on
acquired knowledge of local winds and
currents

USES AND ABUSES

22

1 Speak

Human beings use animals in many different ways for many different purposes, for example: to entertain, to eat. See how many different uses of animals you can think of. The photographs will give you some ideas.

2 Listen

Exam

On tape you will hear different speakers saying something about a particular use of animals. Beside each speaker say what use they are talking about. Fill in F or A in the box to indicate whether the speaker is in favour of or against that use.

a _____ ☐   f _____ ☐

b _____ ☐   g _____ ☐

c _____ ☐   h _____ ☐

d _____ ☐   i _____ ☐

e _____ ☐   j _____ ☐

3 Language
Intensifiers - *rather/quite*

Intensifiers modify adjectives, adverbs, nouns and verbs by indicating the degree.

a How many intensifiers can you think of? Make a list. Are they all interchangeable? Divide them into three categories:
absolute (e.g. *totally*)
high degree (e.g. *very*)
middle/low degree (e.g. *a bit*)

b Listen again to each of the speakers and note the intensifiers and the items they qualify. What parts of speech can we use intensifiers to qualify?

Many adverbs can be used as intensifiers but selecting which one collocates with which word is not always easy. Consider if it is a question of degree or an absolute, for example: *completely finished* not *very finished*. Consider if it has negative or positive connotations. Be careful and look for logical links in meaning.

Put the examples from the tape in three categories (as in a). What is different about *quite* and *rather*?

c What intensifiers can collocate with the following? Think of as many as you can for each.

1 a tired man
2 an arrogant person
3 thoughtfully done
4 educated behaviour
5 contented
6 terrifying

4 Discuss
Consider all the 'uses' of animals. What do you think about each of them? Discuss each 'use' in groups and try to persuade each other that your view is correct.

1 Task

a What is the animal in the photo-graph and what class of animal does it belong to? (For example: reptile). Where do you find it?

b Do you know anything about *continental drift*? Exchange facts and ideas with others.

c Label the following places on the world map. Find out if you do not know.
Kazakhstan   Greenland
South Pole   Scandinavia
South-east Asian Archipelago

2 Read

Read the text.
1 Mark (on the map) where the tooth was found with a **T**.
2 Mark where marsupials originated from with MM.
3 Mark the area/s where placental mammals eliminated marsupials.
4 Mark the two possible routes to Australia.
5 Note which route was thought to be the probable one.
6 Say why the finding of the tooth is so important.
7 Say what use of animals is described here.

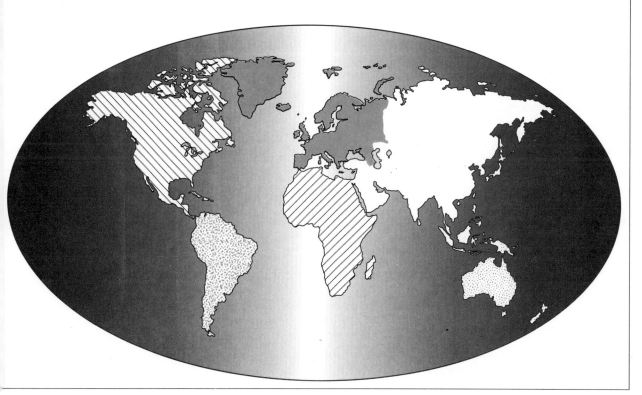

A long hop

IT MUST HAVE been a good deal worse than looking for a needle in a haystack, but a group of scientists working in eastern Kazakhstan has reported an extraordinary discovery in the frozen wastes: a tiny tooth less than 2mm (1/10 inch) across. It is the tooth of a pouched mammal, or marsupial — which would make it the first remains of a marsupial ever to be found in Asia.

The tooth is a first or second upper right molar, the dental experts say — and it is most like that of the extinct opossums called *Amphiperatherium* and *Peratherium*, or the North American *Herpetotherium*. The problem is that its presence reopens an old question: how the marsupials got to Australia?

According to the fossil record so far, marsupials arose in North-west America some 85 million years ago, just 20 million years before the end of the dinosaurs. At the time of the dinosaur catastrophe (possibly caused by the Earth's collision with a comet or asteroid) some three principal Linnaean 'families' of marsupial were flourishing — but only one survived (the opossums).

This reached Europe, as the Atlantic was only just beginning to open in a tearing movement spreading from the south, and the opossums were able to spread across a land bridge from Canada to Greenland to Scotland and Scandinavia.

However, the subsequent European fossil record is fairly scant. Where the marsupials had the time of their evolutionary lives appears to have been South America, where some enormous marsupials including carnivores similar to the placental sabre-toothed tiger emerged. There they flourished until the more efficient placental mammals overtook them. But some reached Australia — where there are now some 13 different families of marsupials — and were saved by continental drift before the placentals could arrive.

But how did the marsupials get to Australia? Before the Australian continent broke loose there were two possible routes: from South America over Antarctica (not then so close to the South Pole), or over Asia from Europe down the archipelago of South-east Asia.

Until the discovery of the Kazakhstan tooth, the Asian corridor was more or less ruled out, as no marsupials had ever been discovered there. But now, on the basis of a tiny piece of dentine, the question must be re-opened.

3 Language
Modal perfects
According to the text, it must have been very difficult finding the tooth. Do we know for certain it was difficult? In whose opinion was it a difficult task? Which words give us this information and which of the following best describe them?

   1 a known fact   2 a logical deduction   3 a guess

speak — making deductions
Make statements based on the information in the text using: must, could, can't, couldn't, have to, might.
For example: *The giant placental mammals must have killed the marsupials.*

Pronunciation
a Listen to the sentences. Each is said twice. What is the change in meaning? What causes the change?

b Listen and match the following phrases to these meanings:

   1 but we didn't try   2 logical truth
   3 possibly difficult but was not   4 I don't believe you

c Practise imitating the pronunciation paying particular attention to the contractions.

Section C

1 Read

Exam

Read the following text. There is an extra word incorrectly added to some lines. Cross these words out.

Human beings' involvement with animals goes to beyond their use as food and clothing. We make toy animals for children and adults; we make food, from breakfast cereals to the chocolates, in the shape of animals; we decorate wallpaper, paint pictures, reproduce photos as posters; but we frequently write stories, as like Rudyard Kipling's *Jungle Book*, and make 5 movies using animals as characters. While therefore many of these are simply light entertainment eg *Bambi* by Walt Disney, there is another form whereby the animal behaviour is has used as a moral lesson. Such allegorical stories are not common in every culture.

2 Language

Giving examples

How do we introduce examples in written language? Look through the text and identify three different ways we can do this in English. Can you think of at least one other way we can introduce examples?

Write a contextualised example sentence for each.

Learner Skills

- identifying use and purpose
- expressing viewpoints for and against
- reading scienfitic text
- relating stress and meaning
- giving examples

Exam Skills

Speaking
A1/4 discussing issues

Listening
A2 matching topic and tone
Exam

Listening
B3 relating tone and meaning

English in Use
C1 proof-reading
Exam

THE DANGERS

23

1 Language
The article
Study the table. Then use a different animal and prepare your own examples for each category. Check your examples.

a + singular noun = one particular one.
A horse was in the field.

a + singular noun = any or all.
A horse makes a neighing sound.

the + singular noun = a specific already defined or identified one.
The horse in the field was galloping about.

the + singular noun = all of this type.
The horse is a noble animal.

the + plural noun = all of those already defined or identified.
The horses in the stables were all ready.

singular noun = all of uncountable mass/stuff.
Hay is the best food...

plural noun = all of this type. ...
food for horses

2 Speak
What is it? Do you like it? What was your first reaction to the photo? How would you feel if you found this in your bedroom? What would you do? Explain your reactions.

3 Read
a Read the poster and the caption. What is a 'deadly beastie'? Why shouldn't people swim where this poster is displayed? Outline what the article will be about.

Exam **b** Read the text and see if your ideas were correct. Choose which of the sentences A-F below match the numbered gaps in the text. There is one extra sentence.

c **Reference.**

1 What is referred to in the text by the following words in italics: *now this*
2 Ring every reference to **the sea wasp**.

Anyone for a swim?: not unless you want to meet this deadly beastie

Beware the killer jellyfish

As of <u>now</u>, and for **the next six months**, it's stinger season in North West Australia.

> **1** [ ]

From October to April, the length of the summer, native Queenslanders either make do with **swimming pools**, wear head-to-toe lycra 'stinger suits' or crowd onto designated beaches protected with mesh netting to keep the killer out.
The sea-wasp, or marine stinger as it's more commonly known, is a small, cube-shaped jellyfish no more than six inches across, but with stinging tentacles that trail several feet from its four corners. During **the winter months** they keep to the narrow creeks and river estuaries that lace this stretch of coastline north of the Tropic of Capricorn, but after the first summer storms, when the sea calms and the water temperature rises, they swarm out along the coast to feed off shoals of shrimp and small fish.

> **2** [ ]

Since they are almost transparent the only sign of their arrival is a bubble-like ripple on the surface as they bob along in search of food.
Rather than drift with the coastal currents like many species of jellyfish, **sea wasps** are agile swimmers and can reach speeds of up to five knots. Their progress is monitored by four main sensory organs that register posture, change of direction and change of light intensity.

> **3** [ ]

They normally try to avoid any dark shapes that approach them, but <u>this</u> is not always possible. Indeed, most fatalities are caused by **swimmers** diving headlong into the water, giving them no chance to get out of the way.
The sting of a sea wasp is agonizing and usually lethal. A stinger no more than three inches across can kill a small child and the larger specimens, with a diameter of up to six inches, can do the same to an adult. **The sting** is delivered by needle-sharp barbs connected to toxin-loaded cells in the tentacles and is triggered by even the gentlest touch. To make matters worse the tentacles often stick to the skin, and the more barbs that make contact, the less chance you have

> **4** [ ]

The poison released by these marine stingers is one of **the deadliest known to man** and, in the worst cases causes death within a matter of minutes. Symptoms include a dramatic rise in temperature, an inability to breathe, blindness and, depending on the degree of exposure, an excruciating death caused as much by the shock of the pain — known to drive victims mad — as

> **5** [ ]

A They particularly favour sandy beaches with no fringing reef or marine vegetation and when the sea is calm they come as close as a few feet from the shore.

B They have a crude "eye" which is capable of forming faint images.

C Shoals of the deadly box jellyfish are making their annual appearance off the coast of Queensland.

D They terrorise Australians with attacks which occur anytime between October and May.

E For this reason Queensland beaches are well stocked with vinegar which, though it doesn't ease the pain, renders the remaining poisonous tentacles inactive.

F Anti-venoms do exist but there is rarely enough time for the victim to be properly and effectively treated.

4 Language

The article
Look at every noun in the article printed in bold.
Comment on the use/lack of article/s in each case. Discuss
difficult ones with the class.

Discourse markers
These are used to hold a text together and to indicate steps
and clarify the argument for the reader.

a In the first two paragraphs, time adverbials are used to
do this. Underline the complete phrases. There are four.

b Locate each of the following markers. What do you
note about their position? What is the meaning of each
in this context:
since   rather   than   indeed   for this reason

Infinitive in initial position
In this example from the text the infinitive clause is placed
before the subject (the tentacles). We do this to focus the
reader's attention on the result of an action.
To make matters worse the tentacles often stick to the skin ...
It is a rather formal pattern and most commonly used in
written language.

Rewrite these examples beginning with the infinitive.

1 He camped nearby so he could investigate the insects
further.
2 She worked with special cameras in order to facilitate
the investigation.
3 He talked to the local people and gained background
information.
4 She learnt some of the language so she could communicate successfully.
5 He threw a party to thank them for their assistance.

5 Vocabulary

a One of the vocabulary sets in this passage is: *the coast
(land and sea)*. Make a list of the words that fit this set.
Compare it with a partner and check you understand
the meaning of each.

b A jellyfish can sting you. What can the following
animals do to you?
a wasp	a dog	a cat	a bee
a spider	a snake	a bat	a mosquito

Section B

1 Speak

Many animals are dangerous to human beings. How many potentially dangerous animals can you name? For each say in what way they can be dangerous. Compare your lists with others.

2 Listen

Exam

You will hear part of a radio programme on dangerous animals. As you listen complete the following notes using a few words. You do not need to write full sentences.

Notes

The naturalist names (1) _____ as being the most famous carnivores. She

gives two examples of killer cats: a lion in Malawi (2) _____ and (3)

_____ responsible for 438 deaths in only 8 years.

After discussing mammals she moves on to (4) _____, giving the first example

of crocodiles which are estimated to be responsible for (5) _____.

In Indonesia, 'the dragon' (a giant iguana) is (6) _____. Recently

(7) _____ by one.

There are about (8) _____ a year from snake bites.

The stonefish is one (9) _____ animals.

The bluefish brings up its food after eating so that (10) _____.

Very often it is not the animal itself which is dangerous but rather

(11) _____.

3 Language

Non-defining relative clauses

a What grammatical differences are there between these two sentences?

Each year there are many deaths which are caused by animals.

There is no real record kept of these deaths, which are numerous.

b Listen to these excerpts from the radio talk and identify the extra information given in non-defining relative clauses.

c Combine the following pairs of sentences into one.

1 The sharks are famous carnivores. Sharks are found all over the world.

2 Most of the cat family will only attack if provoked. The cat family includes puma, lion and domestic cat.

3 The snake is responsible for thousands of deaths each year. The snake is one of the most feared creatures.

Inversion after negative adverbs

The following excerpts from the radio programme are examples of this inversion:

1 Luckily seldom are there such voracious killers.
2 Only recently was a death recorded from a 'dragon' attack.
3 Not only is it employed by snakes but also by spiders.
4 No sooner does it finish eating than it empties its stomach.
5 And while rarely would we have to contend with that today ...

a Study the examples. Mark the inversion. Identify the word/phrase each time which results in the inversion. Rewrite the sentences in a less formal style.

b Two of the key phrases have a second part which is separated from the first. Which are they? Mark the second part in each.

c Write your own example sentences in formal style beginning with the key words. Use the topic of animals if you can.

Section C

1 Task

Prepare an addition to the radio programme.

Step 1 Choose any dangerous animal you know about or you may use the box jellyfish.

Step 2 Note down all the facts that you know. Then organise them into groups, for example: physical environment, food, etc.

Step 3 Decide on the best order for the information and draft your radio script. You may prefer to write only notes.

Step 4 Give your talk. Try to sound as 'expert' as possible.

2 Write

Exam

You have to write an entry for a writing competition entitled *Dangerous Animals*. Your entry should describe the animal, its behaviour and the way in which it is dangerous. You may use your group's notes for information. (200–250 words)

Learner Skills

- reacting and giving reasons
- using and applying your own knowledge
- work on reference
- work on group nouns
- working together and negotiating
- giving talks

Exam Skills

	Speaking
A2	reacting to and discussing a photograph
	Reading
A3b	gapped text
Exam	
	Listening
B2	completing statements
Exam	
	Speaking
C1	long turn speaking
	Writing
C2	descriptive essay writing
Exam	

THE WONDERS

24

1 Read
Read this article. Write a suitable title.

2 Language
Expressing wonder/surprise
Reading about the cane toad eating lighted cigarettes may have surprised you.

What words or phrase could you have used to express surprise or wonder? (N.B. this is positive in attitude not negative as with shock. See page 97.)

Imagine something which surprised or amazed you more. What could you say?

Practise various expressions ranging from mild surprise to total astonishment.

Australia's poisonous cane toad, which devours almost anything in its path, including lighted cigarettes, has been found in Darwin for the first time. The toad was introduced originally in Queensland to control sugar cane parasites.

1 Listen
a Listen to two dialogues. For each dialogue say:
  1 what they are talking about.
  2 what the point of the conversation is.

b Listen again and each time you hear an expression of surprise, write down the actual words.

2 Pronunciation
Study the transcript of the dialogues on page 168.

a In dialogue 1, look at the first line. The new information is *the hoatzin*. Look at lines 4, 7, 8, 12, 13, and 15 and mark the new information in each line. Now listen again and mark the words which are most stressed. What does this tell you?

b Mark the new information in lines 4, 7, 9 and 11 of dialogue 2. Listen and mark the stressed words.

3

These articles are about the animals discussed on tape.

Read one article and complete the grid with information from the text.

	Hoatzin	Orca
Physical features		
Habitat		
Food		
Surprising facts		

Hey, diddle, diddle —
the cow jumped over the Amazon

Wildlife

Robin McKie reports
on an extraordinary inhabitant of the
South American rainforest.

HOATZINS are unusual birds, even for the Amazon forest. They have bright blue faces, big red eyes and orange Mohican hairdoes. Their young swim underwater to avoid predators, and fledglings grow claws and swing through the treetops like monkeys.

It's a formidable combination of talents — though these strange attributes are not the weirdest thing about hoatzins. According to an international group of scientists, the birds also have digestive systems that are the same as cows. A very odd species indeed is thriving in South America, it seems.

These startling avian revelations appear in the current issue of *Scientific American* — and are the work of scientists based in America, Venezuela and Britain.

Thanks to them, the hoatzin's bovine secret has been uncovered — which has at least answered one intriguing puzzle about the birds, their unpleasant smell. (Some Colombians call the bird *pava hidionda* — which, roughly translated means 'stinking pheasant.')

This unpleasant aroma is a feature of their digestive system, it now transpires. Unlike most birds, the hoatzin — pronounced 'WAT-sin', by the way — dines almost exclusively on green leaves. And to cope with this diet, the hoatzin has evolved a digestive system that is unique among birds — but not among cows.

Firstly, swallowed leaves are ground and mashed in the bird's foregut before bacteria ferments this mash to produce nutrients that can then be absorbed in its intestines in the lower part of its digestive system.

Such foregut fermentation is found in cows, sheep, deer and some other mammals, all of which share the same evolutionary pedigree. Hoatzins appear to have developed a bovine-type gastronomic system quite independently. And that, perhaps, is the real puzzle. As the investigators report 'given the abundance of leaves as a resource base, it is not obvious why hoatzins are the only living bird with foregut fermentation.'

Discovering friends in deep places

WHO IS Orcinus Orca, the killer whale or (to Vancouver Island fisherman) the black-fish? Strictly speaking it isn't a whale at all but the largest species of dolphin, though no dolphin has ever been as feared by man.

It is their reputation for devouring seals, sea-lions, porpoises, even other whales, that has earned them the title 'killer'. As with other predators, the diet varies according to habitat. In north-west Canada they compete with fishermen for salmon.

The killer whales of the Island Passage live in family groups (called pods by scientists) of between eight to 15 individuals keeping to reasonably defined areas. They communicate with a complex series of sounds, each pod with a distinctive accent. Killer whales have become the principal attractions at the various Sea World aquariums in the United States, where their performances bring a touch of the circus.

It has not been easy to catch orcas (adults can be up to 30ft long) or to persuade them to live in confinement. In the 1960s, the early captive orcas would refuse to eat, some dying within months, and captive breeding, as with other sensitive creatures of the wild, has had a slow development.

Between 1965 and 1973, 48 killer whales were captured and sold to oceanaria. Paul Spong, a young New Zealand physiological psychologist, was hired by the University of British Columbia in 1967 to study the sensory system of 'Skana', a killer whale at Vancouver Aquarium.

Early one morning, Spong was sitting barefoot at the edge of the pool when Skana, approaching slowly, dragged her teeth across the tops and soles of his feet. He jerked them out of the water until, recovering from the shock, he put them back in. Skana repeated the move. This continued until Spong stopped flinching. Skana desisted and Spong concluded that Skana was conducting an experiment on him.

'Eventually, my respect (for orca) verged on awe,' he wrote. 'I concluded that orcinus orca is an incredibly powerful and capable creature, exquisitely self-controlled and aware of the world around it, a being possessed of zest for life and a healthy sense of humour and, moreover, a remarkable fondness for and interest in humans.'

4 Vocabulary

Scan the article you chose and make a list of words/phrases which express surprise/wonder (for example: *incredibly*).

Work with a partner who read the other article. Add the words/phrases they found to your list and vice versa. Note the part of speech for each word.

5 Speak

Work with the same partner. Exchange information about the two animals using the notes in the grid. Try to exchange as much factual information as you can. As you listen, ask questions about the other animal. Express surprise if you think any of the information unusual.

Section C

1 Read

Exam

a The following article is a factual text giving scientific information about *Fishing spiders*. Read these statements about this spider. Mark the ones you think might be true and the ones you think must be false.

1 Fishing spiders do not actually catch fish.
2 Fishing spiders swim to refresh themselves.
3 Fishing spiders eat insects.
4 Fishing spiders can feel air and water vibrations.
5 Fishing spiders make webs (like other spiders).
6 Fishing spiders are cannibals and eat their own species.
7 Fishing spiders mate many times in their lives.
8 Fishing spider females chase the males.

b Now read the text and find out if your guesses are correct.

2 Language

Discourse markers and textual organisation
Go through the text and underline the word/phrase at the beginning of each sentence. Make a list of these in the order they occur.

1 What is the most common grammatical item?

2 Which of these indicate: time, place, a link in logic?

3 Which could be replaced with *but* and which with *after*?

4 What causes the inversion of verb/subject in the second sentence?

5 Rewrite the second sentence in as many ways as you can (without changing the general meaning). Why did the writer choose the order he did?

6 Rewrite the following sentences: 3, 4, 5 and 8. Express the same ideas.

7 What do *That way* (line 22) and *This* (line 35) refer to?

Spider grabs

Fishing spiders of the genus *Dolomedes* have developed extraordinary skills of water sport. Yet only recently have
5 we learned precisely what *Dolomedes* go swimming for. In small ponds they hunt for insects, mainly on the water's surface, grabbing
10 even the most heavily armoured insect.

But on the shores of lakes and rivers, the bigger spiders attack and kill tadpoles
15 and small fish, such as minnows.

Instead of relying on vibrations on a web to catch prey, *Dolomedes* sense the sur-
20 face waves on the water as well as vibrations in the air. That way they're ready to catch insects swimming, diving, flying or dropping
25 into the water.

In fact, the carnivory of *Dolomedes* is so rampant that five per cent of its total diet is made up of cannibal-
30 ism, with large juveniles and adult females the worst offenders.

Once a female has mated, she doesn't like males any
35 more. This is a problem for the amorous boys, because they don't seem able to tell which are the virgins, so they have a habit of court-
40 ing any female. Yet instead of pouncing on a would-be suitor as soon as he approaches, the mated female seems to feign coy-
45 ness, coaxing the male so near he makes a ridiculously easy victim when she eats him.

3 Write

Write a factual description of any other animal based on the discourse framework of the above article (150–250 words). Choose an animal you know about or collect the necessary information beforehand. Use the list of discourse markers as a framework. It will probably be impossible to use it exactly as it is but try to keep as close as possible and write a descriptive factual piece in formal style.

Learner Skills

- expressing surprise/wonder
- understanding context and purpose
- work on the relationship between sentence stress and given/new information
- guessing as a form of prediction before reading
- work on textual organisation
- working with scientific texts

Exam Skills

A1　*Reading*
selecting title/heading

B1　*Listening*
identifying topic and purpose

B3　*Reading*
extracting factual information from a text and completing grid

B5　*Speaking*
exchanging information

C1　*Reading*
establishing truth of statements from a text

Exam

C3　*Writing*
factual formal writing

EXAM SECTION

ENGLISH IN USE   Section A

Complete the following article by writing the missing words in the spaces provided. Use only one word per space.

Rabid bats out of hell

Gold diggers in Peru are (1) _____ attacked by vampire bats. These are not ordinary vampire bats; these ones carry rabies. No (2) _____ than 24 golddiggers from the town of Puerto Maldonado have died of rabies in the last three weeks, after (3) _____ their blood sucked by vampire bats. A special team of bat-catchers and doctors armed with 11,000 rabies vaccines (4) _____ been sent to the area to try to stop the epidemic spreading.

The bats known locally as "vampiros" have a wingspan of more (5) _____ one metre. They fly into the gold diggers' huts after dark and attach (6) _____ to the sleeping miners heads, necks and feet. The bats' teeth are very small and the victim rarely wakes up. (7)_____ to Dr Hugo Arana, head of the anti-rabies unit in Lima, "The bats also inject an anti-coagulant in their saliva (8) _____ makes the blood flow more freely. This makes the irritation of the bite much (9) _____ ."

He says that normally vampire bats feed on animals (10) _____ probably as a result of the rabies they simply look for the nearest living creature. Dr Arana has plans to catch the bats (11) _____ hanging nets between the trees.

Meanwhile local priests are trying to persuade the miners (12) _____ these attacks are not the work of evil spirits.

WRITING   Section B

You want to contribute to an environmental magazine expressing your own point of view. Write an article (250 words) discussing the advantages and the disadvantages of National Parks. Put the case both for and against protecting our environment and wildlife in this way. Then draw your own conclusions in a final paragraph.

SPEAKING   Phase C

You and your partner have 3 minutes in which to choose which
two of the following visuals to use in a campaign to protect
animal species in danger of extinction. Choose the ones you
think would be the most effective in stimulating public pressure.

WHALE
GOLDEN EAGLE
BENGALI TIGER
AFRICAN ELEPHANT
FEATHER-BACKED TURTLES
GREATER BAMBOO LEMUR
BLACK RHINO
GIANT PANDA
AYE-AYE

ELEPHANT
(EXTINCT)

Mummy, did these really exist?

FINDING OUT

25

1 Read

Many Sunday newspapers in the UK include a colour supplement (a sort of magazine). *The Sunday Correspondent* used to include a particular type of interview more like a questionnaire which attempted to find out some of the more personal aspects of a person's life.

a Read the introductory paragraph about Jessica Catto.
   1 Underline all nouns which are jobs. How many does/did she do?
   2 What would you say is one of her major interests?
   3 Write down 2 or 3 adjectives to describe her.

b Read the questionnaire. Are the following statements True or False about Jessica Catto:
   1 She does not like wildlife.
   2 She admires Cher a great deal.
   3 She prefers dark chocolate.
   4 She admires perfection.
   5 She would like to be able to fly.
   6 She does not enjoy serious reading.
   7 She worries about death.
   8 She really likes the countryside.
   9 She would prefer to be tidier.
   10 She has a sense of humour.

Jessica Catto, 51, the wife of the American Ambassador to Britain Henry E Catto, was born in Houston. Alongside her diplomatic duties she is vice-president of the H & C Communications television company, partner in a Colorado construction company, is building a nature reserve in the mountains near Aspen and is an active trustee of the Environmental Defense Fund. She contributes to the *Washington Journalism Review*, of which she is the former publisher, and the *Washington Post*. The Cattos have four children.

What is your idea of perfect happiness?
A Mountain view, a jug of wine and anything by P D James.

What is your greatest fear?
That mice will get the vote.

With which historical figure do you most identify?
Sacajawea (also known as Bird Woman, Sacajawea was an American Indian guide who carried her infant son on her back across thousands of miles of wilderness with the Lewis and Clark expedition to the Pacific Northwest in 1804).

Which living person do you most admire?
Tina Turner.

What is the trait you most deplore in yourself?
My inability to tell the truth with a straight face.

What is the trait you most deplore in others?
Perfection.

What is your greatest extravagance?
Answering questionnaires.

What objects do you always carry with you?
A calculator and a rabbit netsuke (small pouch).

What are you currently reading?
Citizens: a Chronicle of the French Revolution by Simon Shama.

10 **What makes you most depressed?**
Deprivation of dark chocolate.

11 **What do you most dislike about your appearance?**
The back of my knees.

12 **What is your favourite phrase?**
I agree with you.

13 **Who are your favourite writers?**
Evelyn Waugh and George Eliot.

14 **What is your favourite journey?**
To Eagle (in Colorado, where our ranch is).

15 **Who are your favourite painters?**
Vermeer, Turner and Thomas Cole.

16 **Who are your favourite musicians?**
Puccini and Willie Nelson.

17 **What or who is the greatest love of your life?**
Chico (our dog).

18 **Which living person do you most despise?**
Cher — she is a constant reminder to exercise.

19 **What do you consider the most overrated virtue?**
Neatness — one is not as neat as one would like to be.

20 **On which occasions do you lie?**
During waking hours, and especially when answering questionnaires.

21 **Which words or phrases do you most overuse?**
'Yes' and 'No but'.

22 **What is your greatest regret?**
That I don't look like Audrey Hepburn.

23 **When and where were you happiest?**
In the heather on the hill.

24 **What single thing would improve the quality of your life?**
A magic carpet.

25 **Which talent would you most like to have?**
What, you mean there is something I don't have?

26 **What would your motto be?**
Do unto others ... quickly.

27 **How would you like to die?**
I'll think about that tomorrow.

28 **How would you like to be remembered?**
Often.

29 **What keeps you awake at night?**
Sirens, snores and sighs.

30 **What is your present state of mind?**
Moderate.

c Do you think she answered all the questions seriously? How could you describe some of her answers? Which questions did she answer like that?

2 Vocabulary

a Look through the text and find a word for:
1 *characteristic.*
2 *good characteristic.*
3 *special skill.*
4 *small baby.*
5 *something you can't do.*
6 *wrongly exaggerated.*
7 *dislike intensely/condemn.*

b Write your own example sentences using all the words you have identified. Try to use two or more in one sentence. Compare your sentences with a partner.

3 Listen

Some people were asked questions from the questionnaire. You will hear a selection of their answers to each question, but not the questions. Look back at the text and identify which question was asked each time. Write the question number by each letter.

a ☐   e ☐
b ☐   f ☐
c ☐   g ☐
d ☐

Section B

1 Language

Expressing preference

a In the Catto text, many questions are directed at finding out about her preference or taste. For example: What is your favourite phrase?
1 Identify all the other questions using the same pattern.
2 What other patterns are used for preference?
3 What does *most* qualify in the examples?

b List as many other ways of expressing your taste and preference as you can think of. Give example sentences for each. Compare yours with the class.

2 Listen

a Listen to these dialogues. In each someone expresses a preference. For each one say:
1 whether the situation is formal or informal.
2 where/what is the situation.
3 what the general topic is.
4 what the preference is.
5 what the alternative is.

Fill in your answers on the grid.

b Listen again and write down the actual words used to express the preference each time.

dialogue	formal/informal	situation	topic	preference	alternative
1					
2					
3					
4					

3 Language

To prefer and *would rather*

a Study the examples of each from the previous listening exercise. Separate the *to prefer* patterns from the *would rather*. Identify the grammatical patterns used with the verb *to prefer*. Write your own examples of each. Which patterns do you use to express general preference? And which to express specific preference/choice?

b Study the *would rather* patterns. Work out the different patterns. Write other examples for each.

c Take all your examples and write a negative version of each and an interrogative version of each.

4 Speak

Work in pairs. Tell each other about your taste in all the following: food, sport, movies, books. Talk in general and about specific situations. For example, what do you like to read on planes/on holiday/in bed? Try to use a variety of patterns. Find out if there is anyone else who has the same taste as you for any of the above. Discuss the answers. Which questions provoked the most interesting replies?

5 Task

Step 1 Devise your own questionnaire for finding out about a person. Consider the possible questions you can ask (from the Catto text or your own). Which ones will reveal most about the person? Select about 20 questions. Check the questions for accuracy and organise them into a preferred order. Write a good copy.

Step 2 Interview other people in the room or school using your questionnaire. Each person should interview at least two people.
Discuss the answers. Which questions provoked the most interesting replies?

Step 3 As a class consider all the questions and identify the most revealing ones.

Learner Skills

- analysing an interview
- expressing preference in the present
- devising questionnaire and conducting a survey

Exam Skills

	Reading	
A1b	true/false statements	
Exam		
	Reading	
A1c	reading for tone and style	
	Listening	
A3	multiple match	
	Listening	
B2	interpreting contexts and completing a grid	
Exam		

ONE'S LIFE

26

1 Speak

a Think about this person and their life.
1 What nationality could she be?
2 Where was she brought up?
3 Where has she lived?
4 What has her life been like?
5 What work has she done?
6 Has she been happy/unhappy?

b Compare your ideas about this person and her life. Do you agree?

2 Listen

Exam

Read the following statements about Connie. Listen to the tape and decide if they are True or False.
1 She was unfortunate with her parents.
2 Her parents did not believe in education.
3 In the society she grew up in most people did not educate their daughters.
4 She passed her school exams successfully.
5 She herself applied for a job in the army.
6 She did not take the entrance test seriously.
7 She was not surprised to get the telegram.
8 She did not work for the army for very long.

3 Language
Past preference

There are two possibilities when talking about past preferences.
1 Something preferred which happened.
2 Something preferred which did not happen.

The preference might be:
A For one's self.
B For someone else.

a Study the following examples and state if they are 1 or 2 and A or B.
1 Society preferred girls to stay at home.
2 Her father would rather she had continued her education.
3 Society preferred married women not to work.
4 Her father preferred his daughter to be educated.
5 She preferred to take the job.
6 She would rather not have worked in a hospital.
7 Her father would have preferred her to take other exams.
8 He would have preferred his daughter not to have finished studying.

Which verbs are used to express 1 and which to express 2?
What forms are used to express 1 and 2?
Where does the *not* go in patterns using *prefer*?

b The following table shows the various forms. Complete the gaps for a–f.

	For one's self (A)	For someone else (B)
A preference which happened (1)	a_____ to prefer not to go	to prefer someone to go b_____
A preference which did not happen (2)	would have preferred to go c_____ e_____ would rather not have gone	d_____ would have preferred someone not to go would rather someone had gone f _____

4 Speak

a Consider your own life. Think what preferences your parents had for you and what ones you had for yourself.

b State what your parents preferred for you, what you preferred, what you would have preferred, what they would have preferred. Practise using the different patterns.

5 Write

Exam

The following are the notes for a written report on Connie's life.

Expand the notes into complete sentences and write the text.

-Connie Mark / spend / early years / life / Jamaica

-She / successful / school / pass / exams / continue / study / commercial college

-Though / father / prefer / continue / study / she / work / medical secretary / British Army.

-After / come / UK / 1954 / continue / medical secretary / work / several London hospitals

-Then later / prefer change / job / become / project officer / British Council Aid to Refugees

-Time / she / spend / work / Vietnamese / give / satisfaction

-Despite / broken marriage / Connie / say / lead / same life / again

1 Speak

Make a few notes about your own life. Do not write sentences.

Give a short talk (1–2 minutes) about your life to your class.

2 Write

Exam

When people apply for jobs, they often send a curriculum vitae and a letter of application stating their main reason for applying and identifying their relevant qualifications (including personal attributes).

Study this job advertisement and Valerie Brown's curriculum vitae. Imagine you are Valerie and write her application letter (approx. 250 words). State why you want the job. Give reasons. Show you are appropriately qualified and explain your personal strengths and particular professional areas of interest. Do not write about everything in the cv. Be selective and summarise.

SENIOR NURSERY NURSE

Our well-established nursery (children aged 2–4) requires an experienced, qualified Nursery Nurse. Able to supervise other staff. Must be enthusiastic and imaginative. Apply with C.V. to Rainbow Nursery, Longbrow Avenue, London N.W.6.

Curriculum Vitae

Name:
Address:
Age:
Telephone:

Valerie Brown
64 Shootup Hill, London, NW6
24 years
081 939 6148

Education:
St Mary's High School 1980 – 1986
Harrow Further Education College 1986 – 1988

Qualifications:
GCSE French, English, Hindi, History, Maths, Computer Skills. National Certificate in Nursery Nursing.

Work experience:
Au pair in France –3 children under 5 1988 – 1989

Assistant Playgroup Leader –
Grange Hill Nursery 1990 – 1991

Nursery Nurse –
Peebles Infant School Nursery 1991 – now.

Other skills:
Driving licence, computer literate, good spoken French, knowledge of Hindi.

Interests:
Aerobics, swimming, reading, dancing.

Learner Skills

- expressing past preferences
- comprehending texts for job applications
- writing job application letter

Exam Skills

A1	*Speaking* interpreting photographs
A2 *Exam*	*Listening* true/false statements
A5 *Exam*	*English in Use* constructing text from notes
B2 *Exam*	*Writing* formal letter writing from given information

Me myself

BELIEFS

27

---

1 Discuss

Discuss the people in the photos. Say what they are doing and why.

2 Language
Expressing beliefs

How many words can you build from *believe*? Write example sentences using different grammatical patterns of the words. Check with the rest of the class.

3 Speak

What are your beliefs? What do you believe in? Discuss your ideas and opinions. Use as many of the patterns you can.

Section B

1 Read

Exam

This text is the prologue to an autobiography.

a Consider each of these statements then read the text and find out if they are true. The author
- was superficial.
- hated cruelty.
- had a rich life.
- was depressed all the time.
- never experienced sublime love.
- lived in a fantasy world.
- was studious.
- felt helpless before human suffering.
- went looking for love.
- was cold and distant in personality.

Prologue
What I have Lived for

Three passions, simple but overwhelmingly strong, have governed my life: the longing for love, the search for knowledge, and unbearable pity for the suffering of mankind. These passions, like great winds, have blown me hither and thither, in a wayward course, over a deep ocean of anguish, reaching to the very verge of despair. 5

I have sought love, first, because it brings ecstasy — ecstasy so great that I would often have sacrificed all the rest of life for a few hours of this joy. I have sought it, next, because it relieves loneliness — that terrible loneliness in which one shivering 10 consciousness looks over the rim of the world into the cold unfathomable lifeless abyss. I have sought it, finally, because in the union of love I have seen, in a mystic miniature, the prefiguring vision of the heaven that saints and poets have imagined. This is what I sought, and though it might seem too good 15 for human life, this is what — at last — I have found.

With equal passion I have sought knowledge. I have wished to understand the hearts of men. I have wished to know why the stars shine. And I have tried to apprehend the Pythagorean power by which number holds sway above the flux. A little of 20 this, but not much, I have achieved.

Love and knowledge, so far as they were possible, led upward toward the heavens. But always pity brought me back to earth. Echoes of cries of pain reverberate in my heart. Children in famine, victims tortured by oppressors, helpless old people a 25 hated burden to their sons, and the whole world of loneliness, poverty, and pain make a mockery of what human life should be. I long to alleviate the evil, but I cannot, and I too suffer.

This has been my life. I have found it worth living, and would gladly live it again if the chance were offered me. 30

b Do you think the author was a woman or a man? What job or work did they do? Were they famous? Think of six adjectives which could describe this person. Compare your adjectives with the class.

c The passage contains a mixture of powerful positive and negative images. Identify examples of both. Is the overall effect for you, negative or positive? Say why.

2 Listen

Listen to a short introduction about this person and their life. Make a list of all the factual information. How close was your assessment of this person?

3 Vocabulary

a Find the word/phrase in the text which means:

to give up (in honour)	starvation
the edge (two different words)	to ridicule (to make fun of)
all over the place	to return to reality
a strong desire (noun and verb)	

b Which of the words/phrases do you think are 'poetic'? Which of these items do you think you might use? For every item think of an appropriate situation and give an example.

c We consider words such as: *the, in, would,* and *to be* grammatical words in that they provide a grammatical framework. Think of six other words and compare yours with the class.

We call all other words content words. They convey factual information. For example: *author, passage, write.* Find five content words in the passage which are repeated. Compare yours with the class. Discuss the effect this repetition has.

4 Language

Passage structure

This passage is very logically organised. As a general rule in writing we begin with the general information and then move to the specific.

a The following chart shows how this occurs. Study the chart and the passage and fill in the gaps.

Information Structure

Paragraph 1 topic <u>introduction</u>

1 identification of the three passions

2 statement on the effect of these passions

Paragraph 2 topic _____

1 gives a reason for the first passion

2 gives a second reason

3 gives_____

4 gives a conclusion and result

Paragraph 3 topic <u>second passion</u>

1 relates first and second passions

2 _____

3 _____

4 _____

5 a summary as to the result

Paragraph 4 topic <u>third passion</u>

1 _____

2 states how the third passion had an opposite effect

3 result

4 _____

5 how he feels

Paragraph 5 topic <u>conclusion</u>

1 _____

2 concluding comment

b Look at the second paragraph. What do the first three sentences have in common? Comment on the effect of this feature. Is it (or any similar feature) used elsewhere in the text?

Noun Phrases

Russell used long noun phrases as a (repeated) feature of style of the passage.

List all the noun phrases of three or more words. Which of these have a negative 'feel' to them? Which of them are 'positive' or 'neutral'? Select five phrases which are particularly vivid for you. Check the meaning of all words. Describe the images that the phrases portray for you. Compare your images with others in the class.

Section C

1 Discuss

a Study the collage. For each item say:
1 where you could see it.
2 what its purpose is.
3 which topic it belongs to: love, suffering or knowledge.

b Select one of the three topics. Look back at the relevant photos/texts in the collage. Which do you feel best represent the topic? Which don't? Why? Discuss your views. Think of five other ways to represent the topic visually.

c On the same topic make notes and complete the grid on each of the following:
Think of three things which are true.
For each thing give examples to prove *it is true*.
For each consider the result.

	Truth	Example	Result
1			
2			
3			

d Sit in a group with others working on the same topic. Exchange your thoughts, beliefs and comments. Refer to your notes if you wish. Keep the conversation going for 3–5 minutes.

You could take a lifetime finding the right partner. We may already have found them.
Dateline

I ♥ NY

The Mayfield Clinic

Face lift £2,800.0
Chin tuck £1,500.0
£4,300.

£ 752
£5,05

VAT
TOTAL

Third World Famine
Please give help by sponsoring a little girl or boy in the Third World.
For further information

Improve your memory
and learn a language in a week.
Try our new exciting method of learning.

Please send me my free copy to:

2 Write

Exam

Use your notes and any other ideas and prepare a passage on your topic (approx. 250 words). Reorganise your notes as follows:

Step 1   Paragraph one — The three things.
Paragraph two — examples of the first thing + conclusion.
Paragraph three — examples of the second thing+ conclusion.
Paragraph four — examples of the third thing + conclusion.
Paragraph five — summarising comment/conclusions.
These notes form the basis of your passage. It is now logically organised to follow the principle of 'general to specific'.

Step 2   Write out your notes into a complete passage. Think about textual cohesion: use complex noun phrases and repeat the use of key words/phrases. It is important to think through each idea very carefully. What is the most important element in each? What words best express the idea? How can you say this most effectively?

Step 3   Work through your passage carefully, checking for errors, looking for improvements, making sure each sentence does express what you intended.

Learner Skills

- expressing/understanding beliefs
- interpretation of a text
- lexical cohesion
- understanding textual organisation and cohesion
- understanding context and purpose of texts
- writing essay with structured organisation

Exam Skills

A1	*Speaking*	interpreting photographs
B1a *Exam*	*Reading*	statements from text
B1c	*Reading*	interpreting tone and style
B4	*Writing*	organising text
C1	*Speaking*	exchanging views
C2 *Exam*	*Writing*	discursive essay

EXAM SECTION

SPEAKING   *Paper 5*

Phase A — Social interaction
3 minutes

**Phase B — Information /
Opinion gap**
3/4 minutes

Question 1
Candidate A see page 169.
Candidate B see page 172.

Question 2
Look at the six photographs
on the right.

Candidate A: Listen to your
partner describe one of the
photographs. At the end of a
minute you must say which
photograph has been
described.

Candidate B: Describe one of
the six photographs to your
partner. You have about one
minute to do this.

Phase C
3/4 minutes

Look at the two pictures below. Discuss with your
partner which person has had a better life, which has
achieved more, which has had a better quality of life. You
must either agree with your partner or agree to disagree.
Make sure you understand your partner's opinion. Talk
for about three minutes.

Phase D
2/3 minutes

Give a report/summary of your discussion in C. You may
add further ideas and extend your own opinion.

HOW IT WAS

28

1 Discuss

How important is the environment for good learning/teaching? List what you consider are the 8–10 most important factors in creating a good learning/teaching environment.

2 Listen

Listen to two speakers describe their education.

a Listen to the first description. Note three features about the schooling. Now do exactly the same with the second description. Explain why you chose those particular features. Discuss and compare your choice.

b Listen again. Answer these questions for both speakers.
  1 Where did the speaker go to school?
  2 Was the school single sex or mixed?
  3 Apart from school subjects what other things were taught?
  4 What particular subjects are mentioned?
  5 What other country/ies influenced the education? Why?
  6 In what ways was this influence seen?
  7 What feature would you consider unusual in education?
  8 Think of an adjective to describe how the speaker felt about their education.

3 Discuss

Consider the two schools described.

1 What decades do you think the speakers were referring to?

2 Give your opinion on: the academic education, the 'other things' taught, the attitudes.

3 Was anything similar to your education or anything notably different?

4 Would you have liked to have attended either school? Would you send any of your children to either school? Explain why/why not.

4 Write

Your college is preparing a special magazine on the educational experiences of the students. You have been asked to write an essay describing your own education (approx. 250 words). Choose either your primary or your secondary school.

Section B

1 Speak

Think about both your primary and secondary schools. Were they different or similar? In what ways? What expectations did you have of secondary school? Note five of them. Was it what you expected or different? Describe and explain your expectations.

2 Read

The following two texts are extracts from a novel. They describe a child's experience of their first day at primary school and then at secondary school.

Glossary

slate
thin grey stone used to write on

effaced
rubbed out

hieroglyphics
unintelligible written symbols

yu
you

dilly dally
waste time

bellies
stomachs

Little Boy Blue and Little Miss Muffet
two nursery rhymes

haystack
large pile of hay firmly packed for storing

On my first day at school Mrs Hinds called to me to come to her with my slate. Across the top of it she made a row of identical creatures and handed slate and pencil back to me saying: 'Here, make A for Apple,' and took up her embroidery again. I went back to my place and after a few moments of bewilderment followed my neighbour's example in filling up the whole slate with things of the approximate shape of those made by Mrs Hinds.

Everybody else was scraping away at their slates, and occasionally someone effaced their hieroglyphics with a liberal wash of water (or spit) and then waved their slate about in the air singing:

> *Fumbie Fumbie dry mih slate*
> *I'll give yu a penny toba-cco*

and often slates tended to be waved smack into neighbour's faces, which tended to generate loud strife. Everybody seemed to know what they were about, everybody seemed to be in the middle of something.

My reading career also began with A for Apple, the exotic fruit that made its brief and stingy appearance at Christmas-time and pursued through my Caribbean Reader Primer One the fortunes and circumstances of two English children known as Jim and Jill, or it might have been Tim and Mary.

At about twelve o'clock we sang grace, 'Hands together, eyes shut!' and anyone caught with so much as one eye half-open receiving a sound slap. Then we scampered out, with admonitions from Mrs Hinds to 'Go straight home, don't dilly-dally on the way!'

On afternoons the tempo was slow. Lunch was still heavy in our bellies, the sun which had battered down at us on the way back to school was still outside besieging the walls, cooking the air inside the schoolroom, and everyone felt most like sleeping. So we stood and counted in unison to a hundred, or recited nursery rhymes about Little Boy Blue (what, in all creation, was a 'haystack'?) and about Little Miss Muffet who for some unaccountable reason sat eating her curls away.

Read the first passage and answer these questions by choosing the best alternative.

1 Mrs Hinds made a row of
  A animal pictures.
  B the letter A.
  C letters.
  D apples.

2 The child felt
  A puzzled.
  B interested.
  C horrified.
  D worried.

3 The children dried their slates
  A by saying rhymes over them.
  B by wiping them on each other's clothes.
  C by waving them in the air.
  D by waiting.

4 Arguments arose because
  A the children didn't know what to do.
  B the teacher paid no attention.
  C they sometimes hit each other with their slates.
  D they were bored.

5 Reading was taught
  A from religious books.
  B from books about Caribbean life.
  C from books about apples.
  D from books about life in England.

6 In the afternoon the children wanted
  A to play.
  B to sleep.
  C to go home.
  D to sing nursery rhymes.

7 Physical punishment
  A was used for discipline.
  B was very rare.
  C was extremely harsh.
  D was forbidden.

8 In this primary school, the children
  A worked very hard.
  B did exactly as they wanted.
  C learnt nothing at all.
  D managed to learn something.

3 Vocabulary

All the following verb phrases occur in the first passage.

to call to	to fill up
to come to	to scrape away
to hand back to	to wave about
to take up	to be about
to go back	to batter down

a Find the example of each and where appropriate complete the infinitive verb phrase, for example: *to call someone to something*. Try to work out the meaning from the context. Use a dictionary if you wish.

b For each verb write an example sentence exemplifying the same meaning but in a different context.

4 Read

Now read the same author's description of secondary school.

a Read the first paragraph. What did she expect? Was it like that? In what way was it different from her expectations?

b Read the second and third paragraphs and draw a sketch of what the school looked like.

c Read the fourth and fill in the missing prepositions.

Big-school lived up to a great deal of our mixed expectations. Much of it was the purest exhilaration, like the feel of the crisp new copy-book with the King's head on the outside and the neat pattern of blue and red lines on the inside waiting to be overrun by the new scholarship. But there was so much we had not altogether bargained for - a teacher who was an individual who kept a sharp eye on you all the time, neither embroidering nor chatting with her mother; the menace to life and limb constituted by the presence of hordes of older children. Too much of Big-school, it seemed, was going to be sheer dismay.

We sat in a kind of well, for there were children packed onto a raised platform running around the edges of the cavernous hall that had a continuous wire-netting slit along the tops of its walls, like lavatory windows letting in dusty light in a chequered pattern over our heads. The well was filled in with a bizarre patchwork of children in thick squares that were closely wedged together but facing different directions and reciting and buzzing in contradictory tempos. Morning assembly was an uncomplicated process - we merely stood up in our places and faced one end of the hall, and when it was over we turned to our proper directions and sat down again. The whole school could never be got onto one floor, so Mr Thomas held assembly upstairs while Teacher Iris led the prayers downstairs. The problem of synchronizing the singing was given much thought and effort, but still the upstairs assembly always managed to be a line or two behind us in the hymn, so that the total effect was something in the nature of an ecclesiastical rendition of Three Blind Mice.

In the beginning the thought of all those children was alarming. There was our multitude, the lowest classes, 'down-on-the-ground' as the others said with a certain contempt. We were surrounded by the condescending benches of bigger children ranged on the platform. And over our heads every time the bell rang, was the most terrifying thunder of feet and furniture, reminding us that upstairs were just as many children again as we could see around us, bigger and more condescending yet than the ones up on the platform.

Big-school was no place (1) ___ little children. At recess-time the upstairs children materialized like doom hurtling down the back and front stairs which could barely contain the torrent. The whole building seemed (2) ___ tremble. Outside we clung to the walls and hovered (3) ___ sheltered places for fear (4) ___ being knocked down and trampled upon (5) ___ the giants galloping about their yard. The four standpipes were permanently surrounded (6) ___ a knot of viciously jostling children so that there was almost no chance (7) ___ us ever getting a drink of water — sometimes a bigger brother or sister would push one of us (8) ___ to the tap but the younger children as often as not emerged in tears, dishevelled and drenched.

5 Language

Past expectations *was going to*

This is another form of future in the past which we use to express an expectation, for example:

The child thought secondary school was going to be wonderful but after one day she realised *too much of Big-school … was going to be sheer dismay.*

In what ways was it going to be sheer dismay? Write three examples each beginning: *She thought that …*

6 Vocabulary

The novel is written in a very rich style using many adjectives and descriptive verbs.

a In the second passage many of the words and phrases emphasise the physical activity and the resultant danger to smaller children. For example: *exhilaration, to over-run, a menace to life and limb.*

Find the above expressions in the text and make a list of all other words/phrases which create this effect.

b Select five new words/expressions to learn and write example sentences.

7 Pronunciation

a Listen to the first two paragraphs of the second passage read aloud. As you listen mark the pauses (/). Remember how each chunk of text usually contains one piece of information and that one (or two) words are stressed more than others.

b Study the third and fourth paragraphs. Divide the passage into chunks and mark the words to be stressed.

Listen to the paragraphs read aloud and see if your chunks are similar. Discuss any differences with your teacher.

Learner Skills

- discussing, assessing, negotiating as speaking skills
- expressing past expectations
- understanding the value of lexical cohesion
- work on information chunks and stress

Exam Skills

	Listening
A2b	detailed factual listening
	Writing
A4	descriptive essay
Exam	
	Reading
B2	multiple choice
Exam	
	English in Use
B4c	gap filling exercise

HOW IT IS

29

---

1 Discuss

Exam

Work in pairs. A look at photo 4 on page 171. B at the photo 8 on page 172. Describe the photos to each other. Identify any similarities/differences. One of you will report your conclusions to the class.

2 Listen

Exam

Listen to a teacher, Sue Bent, explaining the *thematic approach* to teaching. She is talking specifically about a class of 8/9-year-olds. As you listen, complete the grid.

Compare and exchange your information with a partner.

What, does she say, is the reason for the success of the *thematic approach*?

Subjects	Last term	This term
	Theme: *light and colour*	Theme: *transport*
language		Integrated across curriculum Spelling sheets of related words
maths	1_____	Special lessons less related - except thirds re icebergs
science	2_____ prisms rainbows	How things move on land, sea + air
environmental studies	3_____ cars	
history		4_____ Social aspect of classes.
geography		5_____ (journeys)
religious education	Rainbows in different religions	Journeys in religions/ type of transport
art	6_____	7_____

1 Read

The children wrote about their wishes.
Read the notes and:
1 list all their wishes.
2 make a note of the *I wish* patterns
they use.

One piece contains errors in grammar.
Which is it? Correct the errors.

2 Language

Expressing wishes and regrets

a What is the difference between
saying:
I wish dreams would come true and
I wish my aunt had not died.

b Which of these are regrets and which
are wishes?
1 I wish the world was a better place.
2 I wish the Titanic had not sunk.
3 I wish we could fly.
4 I wish they would invent a non-
polluting car.
5 I wish I had a baby brother.
6 I wish there was no fighting in the
world.
7 I wish I had a pony with bright
coloured wings.
8 I wish it was like in the olden days.

c Look at all the wishes. What tense is
used in 1, 6 and 8? What alternative
would fit? Which other examples use
this tense? Contrast these examples
with those using *would* and *could*.
What is the difference?

d What is an alternative way of saying
I wish?

3 Speak

Think of your own life. Think of five
things you regret and five things you
would wish for. Use a variety of patterns.
Compare your wishes/regrets. Can you
find anyone with any of the same regrets
or wishes?

1 I wish I had lots of money and a big house. I wish the world was not polluted and it was like in the olden days. I wish my brother would not climb on me. I wish my brother could play with me.

2 I wish I had the whole set of Action Force. I wish I had five big brothers. I wish I was an expert at surfing. I wish my Dad was more playful.

3 I wish that nothing would happen to my family. I wish I was the fastest man in the whole world. I'd wish Ethiopia wasn't poor any more in their life time. I'd wish everybody will keep the British Isles tidy. I'd wish everybody will stay young then nobody will die.

4 I wish everyone was peaceful. I wish people would share and care for everyone. I wish people would stay and never die. I wish dreams would come true and the last thing I wish is for everyone to be happy.

Section C

1 Listen

Exam

Listen to the teacher's comments on some of the children's work.

The following notes summarise her comments. Complete the notes from listening to the tape. You may use one or more words in each blank but you do not need to write full sentences.

SUE BENT - COMMENTS

The main benefit from drawing the pictures **1** _____ afterwards.

The oral description of the pictures **2** _____ they had done that term. Another very important aspect was **3** _____ and **4** _____ which had taken place initially. Groupwork encourages them to **5** _____ as well as express their own. It is important to stimulate **6** _____ allowing them to fantasize. Another fundamental aim was to get the children thinking of **7** _____ , to go beyond their limits of home **8** _____ . This is reflected in their **9** _____ which range from **10** _____ to the political.

---

2 Language

should have

Study these two sentences. Is there a difference?

They should've learnt quite a lot of language from writing instructions.

They should've gone to visit the Transport Museum.

a Did they write instructions? Did they learn language? What is the speaker's opinion?

b Did they go to the Transport Museum? What is the speaker's opinion?

3 Speak

Give as many answers as possible to the following questions.

1 What should Sue Bent's class have learnt from their studies of light and colour?

2 What should have been done to improve your schooling?

Learner Skills

- discussing issues and approaches
- discussing and analysing opinions
- expressing wishes, regrets and expectations

Exam Skills

	Speaking
A1	information gap
Exam	
	Listening
A2	grid completion
Exam	
	Listening
C1	text completion
Exam	

HOW
IT SHOULD BE

30

1 Speak

What do you think children's education really should be like?

a Consider:
the environment
the teacher
the relationship with students
the subjects
the teaching methods
the attitudes

b List the five most important qualities for each of:
a good teacher, a good student, a good teaching method, a good school.

c Discuss all the qualities you have listed then agree on the five most important for each topic.

2 Listen

Listen to a variety of individuals express their views on education in the future. Some have a positive and some a negative attitude.

1 Match each speaker to a topic (write speaker number).

2 State if the speaker is positive or negative (write P or N).
Discuss your opinions and check your answers with the class.

3 Language
The future

Listen again to the tape.

a List all the examples where the speaker refers to the future.

b Identify which patterns express:
future obligation, future prediction, future wish, future query.

c Analyse the verb forms and name the tenses.

d For each pattern and function (see b) write your own example sentence.

Topic	1	2
discipline	☐	☐
internationalism	☐	☐
education for all	☐	☐
danger of too much	☐	☐
schooling at home	☐	☐
basic survival	☐	☐
environment	☐	☐
computers	☐	☐

4 Speak

a Think about the following questions about education in the year 2500.
What will it be like?
Where will children spend the day?
What will they be doing?
Will everything be computerised?
Will they have stopped doing certain subjects like arithmetic?
Who will be doing the teaching?
How will schooling be organised?
How would you like to see education developing?

b Working in groups, summarise your speculations. Try to agree between you on the future of education. Appoint a spokesperson to report on your discussion to the class.

Section B

1 Discuss

Think about these headlines to two newspaper articles; both are concerned with a move towards international education. Discuss them and say what each could be about. Compare your ideas.

Text 1 **Goodbye High School, hello Africa**

Text 2 **First class to New York**

2 Read

Skim read these cut-up sections and decide if each is Text 1 or Text 2. Then sort them out into the correct order.

GCSE and A-levels are U.K. examinations taken at approximately 16 and 18 years of age.

20 Lucy Delap is 17, English and has a complaint common to many British school pupils: when she goes to school in the morning it is frequently cold, and so misty that she can barely see her classroom in front of her.

3 Language

Textual cohesion and coherence
Study your joined up text. Number the joins 1–9 for each article. Look at each join and decide if there is a language link demonstrating cohesion. Identify the link. If there is not, say why the two pieces join. Is it purely logic demonstrating coherence?

7 Every morning when he arrives at school, 10-year-old Gavin Cooper checks the mailbox to see if there are any messages from his schoolfriends in the US.

10 Nothing unusual about that, except that the mist is on a mountainside in Mbabane, the capital of Swaziland.

Lucy sat 10 GCSE's at Aleyn's High School in Dulwich last year and everyone presumed she would make the natural progression to A-levels. However, she had other ideas: a friend had told her about a school in Swaziland called Waterford Kamhlaba

3 you are helping people directly and not just being a spectator.'

Awareness of the political situation in South Africa is an integral part of life at Waterford and Lucy finds this one of the most satisfying aspects of the college. 'My ideas about South Africa were very vague when I arrived here but already they are much clearer. Sixty per cent of the students here are South Africans,

4 and sent over their thoughts for discussion by their friends. Rising interest rates, Hillsborough and train derailments were subjected to the scrutiny of 10 and 11-year-olds. The two schools are also planning to work together on a conservation project and Sybil Camsey is hoping to display the Bronx work alongside that of her pupils.

The project's enhancement of the curriculum is heightened by the fact that while Barnehurst is a mainly white school in a fairly prosperous district PS122 has 1400 pupils, is in a poor area, and has a 70 percent Hispanic, 28 percent black intake. The Bronx children chosen to take part in the link have above-average reading levels.

Sybil Camsey finds it impossible to hide her excitement about potential benefits. The New York club, she says, is an excellent way of stretching the school's more able children.

9 and then send it to the Bronx. The older children train the younger ones so that the project can continue smoothly.

During the summer term, Barnehurst and PS122 took it in turns to choose items of news which interested them

12 than a separate subject of study.

For Barnehurst, D-Day was back in February although, like all schools in the project, the pupils had first exchanged a welcome package with their link school including writings, drawings and photos of the school and themselves.

Sybil Camsey, deputy head at Barnehurst

16 It is financed by the National County Council for Educational Technology and co-ordinated by the South Bank Polytechnic, which has linked 24 primary, secondary and special schools in and around London with a similar number in New York.

John Meadows, co-ordinator at the South Bank, hopes that the project will lead to an evaluation of whether such links are worthwhile and at the same time encourage the use of computers in the school and community as a tool rather

13 all of which follow the IB and are open to anyone regardless of race, colour, creed or ability to pay as UWC will sponsor anyone who is chosen but cannot afford the fees.

Lucy wrote to UWC in London and was invited to its college in Wales for a weekend of personality tests and group discussions.

11 Another important aspect of the IB syllabus is its emphasis on community service. Before Waterford, Lucy's only experience of this was visiting an elderly lady in London who died a week after her first visit. Now she spends three hours a week looking after children in a local hospital.

'It can be quite harrowing because of the lack of equipment and facilities but in a way that makes you feel more useful. Doing community service in a Third World country you know

5 that follows the International Baccalaureate (IB) syllabus and is multi-racial — a significant feat considering it is surrounded on three sides by South Africa. Waterford is run by the United World College (UWC), an organisation that has seven colleges worldwide,

was still learning to find her way around the computer when day one arrived. Contact was made. 'Surprise, surprise. We switched on our computer, pressed all the right buttons. And there it was. A letter from the New York teachers. 'Our children are on holiday until next week

of all colours, so we hear all the points of view. It has made me realise how little we really know in Britain about South Africa.'
Lucy says she has been too busy to be homesick. I can vouch for this: I spent one day there as a spectator and collapsed exhausted into bed, with the mist rolling in over the mountain,

4 find access to their computer more difficult.
The technical hitches have now been ironed out. The New York club operates all day on Friday, when the children discuss what they are going to say to their American friends, write and edit on the word processor, store the work on disc,

The knowledge that their opinions are directed at an interested audience extends their level of thought and vocabulary. The word-processor frees them from the mechanical chore of writing. Their only limitation is the number of computers.

while Lucy and her fellow IB students were enthusiastically rehearsing a production of Measure for Measure.

1 He usually has a younger pupil in tow who is learning some of the technological intricacies Gavin takes for granted.
For this is no ordinary mailbox. Seventeen fourth-year pupils at Barnehurst Junior School in Erith, Kent, are involved in a pilot project using electronic mail to link their school with one in New York.
The Global Project has been running for nearly two years.

15 but will write as soon as they get back. It is five o'clock in the afternoon here and just getting dark.'
Once the Barnehurst children were on-line, interest in the New York club, as they call it, snowballed. In theory the children could have an instant electronic dialogue with their link school, PS122 in the Bronx. But the time difference means there is only one hour a day when both sets of pupils are at school. Barnehurst is fortunate in having five computer work-stations, including one with the necessary modem. Their Bronx counterparts

18 but Lucy sees it as a chance to extend both her social and educational horizons.'There are students from 45 countries at Waterford and because of the variety everyone is open-minded and friendly: I felt at home after only one week. It also gives you a more balanced view of the world, not just the British one.

'When I left my school in England my headmaster said that I was leaving the mainstream of education, but I think the opposite is true. In the IB syllabus we do six subjects, three at a higher level and three at subsidiary level so there is a much wider range than A-levels as we study all these subjects for two years. Also, we can go to universities all over the world with our IB certificates.

17 Of 3,000 applicants, 75 were interviewed for 18 places in the seven colleges. Lucy passed the test. Initially her friends at home wondered why she wanted to go to a largely unknown syllabus

Section C

1 Read

Now read and list the advantages to the children of both schemes.

2 Vocabulary

a Scan the articles and find all the vocabulary items connected with **education**. Arrange them in lists according to their parts of speech. Compare your lists with others and discuss any problems.

b Select five different items which are unknown to you. Find out their meanings then write your own examples.

3 Discuss

Look at your list of advantages (C1). Do you think they are advantages? Compare your opinions. List all the disadvantages of these schemes you can think of. Assess the value of both schemes. Report your conclusions to the class.

4 Write

Refer to the two articles and to your discussion to consolidate your ideas.

Write a letter to the editor of the newspaper in response to the two articles (approx. 250 words). In the letter you should express your opinion of the value (or lack of it) of both schemes. Give your reasons. Refer to any particular points. You may also say something about how you see internationalism in education and give your ideas for education in the future.

Learner Skills

- negotiating
- analysing functions of language
- work on textual cohesion and coherence
- identifying advantages and disadvantages
- assessing value of proposals

Exam Skills

A1	*Speaking* negotiating, assessing
A2 Exam	*Listening* interpreting tone and topic match
A4	*Speaking* summarising and reporting spoken discussion
B2	*Reading/English in Use* working with gapped texts
C3	*Speaking* reporting on discussion
C4 Exam	*Writing* writing letter to newspaper

EXAM SECTION

ENGLISH IN USE   Section C

You have been asked to write a handout for new and inexperienced teachers from the point of view of the students in a school.

You have made some initial notes on which to base your handout. You may add words and change the form of words where necessary. The first point has been expanded for you as an example.

To all new teachers
We, the students have put together some guidelines which should help you to enjoy your teaching.

a *Try to make the work interesting and challenging*
  That way ...
  _____
  _____

b _____
  _____

c _____
  _____

d _____
  _____

e _____
  _____

f _____
  _____

g _____
  _____

h _____
  _____

a make work interesting/challenging -
   achieve best results/response students
b set homework - give typed copy to all
c mark homework - positive/negative
   comments so aware strengths and
   weaknesses. Return promptly
d provide handouts/notes - accompany
   lectures
e write board - try clear + legible/
   organised. Give time - copy.
f if student difficulty - help
g listen us, adult human beings - treat so
   - then all benefit
h enjoy teaching - we enjoy learning

LISTENING   Section D

You will hear three people expressing their opinions on education —
why it is important and what makes a good education. You will hear
the tape twice.

Task One
Letters **A-H** list the essentials of a good education. As you listen mark
which speaker, 1, 2 or 3, mentions which of the options. Some of the
options will be used more than once, some not at all.

Task Two
Letters **I-N** list the reasons for the importance of education. As you
listen mark which speaker, 1, 2 or 3, gives which reasons.
Some reasons will be used more than once, some not at all.

List A: Essentials of a good education

A   motivated students   ☐

B   interesting classes   ☐

C   good materials   ☐

D   individual development   ☐

E   good teacher   ☐

F   discipline/hard work   ☐

G   challenging/stimulating   ☐

H   good environment   ☐

List B: Reasons for the importance of education

I   to make a career   ☐

J   to understand and relate to others   ☐

K   to lead a full life   ☐

L   to get qualifications   ☐

M   to meet society's demands   ☐

N   to face responsibilities   ☐

WRITING   Section A

You joined a course in Tourism in September this year. However you and your fellow students are not very satisfied with the course. You held a course meeting at which notes were made as to the main problem areas. You have been asked to write the letter on behalf of all the students to the College Principal outlining your complaints and asking for improvements to be made for the remainder of the course.

Write the letter to the Principal using the information given below. Use an imaginary address for yourself. Date the letter appropriately. You may invent any necessary extra details to complete your answer provided that you do NOT change any of the information given.
You are advised to write approximately 250 words.

General Certificate in Tourism

An introductory course leading to a qualification widely recognised within the industry. The course (20 hours per week) lasts a full academic year. Students are awarded the Certificate on the combination of 60% course work and 40% final written examination.

Course Content

• 10 core subjects studied for different periods of time. Including marketing, finance, management, computer technology.

• Regular visits to places of interest, eg tourist venues, information offices.

• Three weekends' work experience each term for each student in appropriate organisations.

• Eight assignments over two terms (four each) plus individual projects in the third term. Marks awarded are worth up to 60% of the final assessment.

• Access to college computers for working outside course hours.

• Option of taking a foreign language as an additional component.

Student Meeting - 21 November
Points to Raise

A course meeting - all attended - the following all agreed on ....

-Assignments   three set and handed in so far this term ... none returned. Cannot know how we're doing ... what progress ... what to improve...

-Marketing   lecturing not up to standard ... always late ... poorly prepared ... little challenge in the work ... lack of hand-outs/bibliographies.

-No visits at all this term ?????

-Work Experience   5 people still not had placements ... !! 3 of the other 8 were extremely unsatisfactory - free labour/no learning - waste of time, overall lack of planning and organisation in this area.

-Foreign Languages   No option given ... no information ... !!

-Some aspects fine particularly computer technology and help from staff... also management.

Harry Worth College

High Road, Elmslow, Wicks. WA3 2YZ.
Principal: Mrs Jasmine Bent

```
Policy on Standards

We aim to run all our courses at a very
high standard. In order to help us
maintain those standards we do invite
students to comment. Positive comments as
well as negative comments are welcome. If
students do feel that they have problems
with a particular course they are
requested to put this in writing. The
Principal has the right to call meetings,
hold investigations, interview students
and staff alike. Any steps taken will be
at the Principal's discretion.
```

ENDMATTER

ref: page 104

ref: page 129

Text 1

The Jim Twins

Jim Lewis and Jim Springer had been separated when they were four weeks old and adopted into different families. When they were reunited at the age of 39, it was found that their new lives had similarities. Here are just a few.

1 Both had married a girl called Linda, divorced her and then married a Betty.
2 Both had dogs called Toy.
3 Lewis called his first son James Alan, Springer called his James Allan.
4 Both had worked in MacDonalds, also as petrol pump attendants, and both had a stint as deputy sheriff.
5 Both had the same make of car and drove it to exactly the same beach for their holidays each year.
6 Both bite their fingernails to the quick, and chain smoke.
7 Both have sleeping problems, suffer migraines and have had two heart attacks.
8 Both had built white benches around the trunk of the tree in their gardens.

Dialogue 1

```
A  Have you ever heard of the
   hoatzin?
B  The what?
A  The hoatzin, well I think that's
   how it's pronounced.              5
B  Well, I haven't.
A  Actually it's a bird. It's South
   American and it smells.
B  Yuck! Are you going to tell me
   why?                             10
A  You won't believe this but it's
   got a stomach like a cow.
B  It's what!
A  Yeh and its babies have claws and
   hang around in the trees like    15
   monkeys.
B  Go on, you're pulling my leg!
A  Here you are. Read it for
   yourself!
C  I can't get over how intelligent  20
   they are.
D  Well so I've heard but... what
   proof is there?
```

Dialogue 2

```
C  Oh, I heard about some guy who
   swears that the whale actually
   performed experiments on him!
D  Really! And just how?
C  I'm not sure of all the details    5
   ... but if it's true then ...
D  Wasn't there a Star Trek movie
   about rescuing whales from now
   from our time and taking them into
   the future?                      10
C  'Cos they've got some secret and
   the world can't exist without
   them.
D  Seems a bit far fetched but then
   they're pretty amazing creatures. 15
```

QUESTION 1

Candidate A: Describe the picture to your partner who has a picture which is related to yours in some way. You have about 1 minute to do this. Your partner will then tell you two things which are the same and three which are different.

ref: page 150

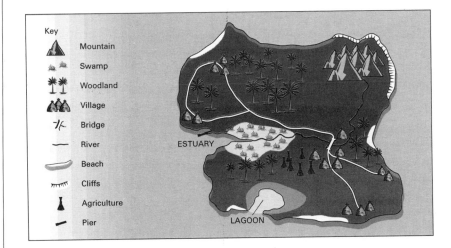

ref: page 46

ref: page 114

a

I was on holiday in what is now Namibia and I was driving with some friends along this road. Namibia is a
very desolate country and you go for hundreds of miles
along straight roads and I was driving along this
straight road and right into the sun even though I had
the shades down and everything else you couldn't... and
I actually experienced this thing of actually blanking
out and the next thing I knew I was ploughing across
the open bush and it was a really horrific experience
because one moment I was along this road and the next
moment I was somewhere else and it was really quite a
strange experience and the heat and the light...

b

When I was a boy we lived in Islington which was quite
a run down area in those days and my mother used to
take my younger brother and I to the market when we
were about 4 and 3 and she always used to lose us. The
first time this happened she was very distraught. She
went to the police station and asked, have you got two
little boys called Sean and Hugh Byrne here? and the
police lady was very sorry but she didn't. They only
had two little boys in there and they went by the
names of Bill Badger and Edward Trunk. ... After a few
minutes my mother went in the room and collected us.

c

This concerns a frightening experience I had when I
was about 15. I was working in an after school job as
a cleaner in a furniture factory and in this big factory everyone had gone. It was empty and a storm
started to blow up and everything started rattling and
I was getting fairly spooked anyway and it grew darker
of course and suddenly there was this very loud bang-
ing noise where this door behind me had slammed shut
and I span around to see this man standing across from
me about 5 feet away with a broom held in a fairly
aggressive position. A few seconds later I realised it
was a full length mirror and I was just about to
attack myself.

ref: page 58

ref: page 157

ref: page 46

Question 1:

Candidate B: Look at the picture which is related in some way to your partner's picture. Listen carefully and then tell your partner two things which are the same and three things which are different.

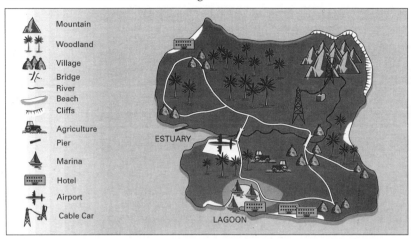

ref: page 150

ref: page 58

ref: page 157

ref: page 41

Stephanie   Best friends... I think that they're very important in most people's lives. If you don't have a best friend you don't... and you can't talk to a sister or a brother it's like something's missing out of your life, you have to talk to somebody about your problems at home, about boys, about or girls if you're a girl, a boy... and if you don't have a best friend I think you feel very lonely basically that's about it really.

Jeremy   Best friends... best friends are people who you can usually ring up at the most impossible hours if you have a problem. Best friends I find that I have one or two very very good friends. We don't always see each other that often but somehow when we do meet we can get into sort of quite serious, quite deep sort of conversation without having to go through all this social chit-chat, you can get down to the nitty gritty and we seem to be able to pick up you know the threads of our lives, you know quite quickly.

ref: page 104

Text 2

Michael and Alex

When Michael joined the navy at 16, his identical twin brother, Alex, came to see him off. Four days later, when Alex was celebrating New Year's Eve at a friend's house, he complained of tiredness and went to lie down. He died a couple of hours later of a heart attack. When his twin heard the news he immediately cabled home, but that night he too died in his sleep, 48 hours after his brother.

Keith and Kenneth

Keith and Kenneth were also identical twins. Keith had a hole in the heart and was admitted to Newcastle hospital to have an exploratory operation. At 12.15 that day, Kenneth suddenly broke down in tears complaining of pains in the chest. This was the exact same time that Keith was on the operating table.

GRAMMAR REVIEW

CONTENTS

Verbs and verb patterns

There are two types of verbs in English: main and auxiliary.

Main verbs
These can be either regular: *to call* or irregular: *to write*.
The main verb has five forms:
1 the infinitive with *to*: *to call, to write*
   or infinitive without *to* (the stem): *call, write*
2 the *-s* form: *calls, writes*
3 the past: *called, wrote*
4 the *-ing* participle: *calling, writing*
5 the participle: *called, written*

State and event verbs
There are two categories of main verbs:
1 State verbs. These describe a state, and most cannot be used with the progressive aspect: *I know Jim.*
2 Event verbs. These describe either an event: *It happened last night.* Or a series of repeated events: *She went to school every day.*

Verb phrases
A verb phrase is any phrase which begins with a verb. It may be one word or more. It may contain two, three or more verbs and is either finite or non-finite.

Order of verbs in verb phrases
Rules determine the possible combinations when there is more than one verb in a verb phrase. For example:

| He | may | have been | seen. |
| | modal auxiliary | passive *be* | main verb |

The finite verb phrase has a tense and agrees with the subject.
   She works very long hours.
   Before he had finished he phoned the office.
The non-finite verb phrase uses the verb either:
● in the infinitive: *To work like that is crazy.*
● as a present participle: *Before finishing, he called her.*
● as a past participle: *Lived in by many, the house was old.*

Verb patterns
The structural pattern which follows a verb is determined by the verb itself. There are six basic patterns, each with variations, and some verbs can be used with more than one pattern. When you learn a new verb always make a note of the full pattern. A dictionary will tell you this. For example:
   to persuade someone to do something
not just *to persuade*
Use these abbreviations:
s/o = someone *s/thg* = something

Auxiliary verbs
Auxiliary verbs help to form a tense and/or establish mood or attitude. They usually form part of a verb phrase together with a main verb.
The principal auxiliaries are: *do, have, be.*
The modal auxiliaries are: *can, could, may, might, shall, should, will, would, must, ought to.*
The semi-modal auxiliaries are: *need, dare, used to.*

Time and tense

One way of looking at tenses is to start from the idea that there are two basic tenses in English, the Simple Present and Simple Past.

Simple Present
Form *I walk   he/she/it   walks*
Use   The Simple Present is used for: a state, an event, a habit, and a factual future.

Simple Past
Form *I walked*
Use   The Simple Past is used for: a definite state, event or habit which is clearly identifiable as being in the past.

Other tenses are formed by combining these two basic tenses with two aspects, the progressive and the perfect.

The Progressive aspect
Form The progressive aspect is formed with *be* + verb + *-ing*.
The Present Progressive (Continuous) *I am working in hospital.*
The Past Progressive (Continuous) *I was living in London then.*

Use   The progressive aspect conveys the concept of temporariness. This means that it is most commonly found with event verbs.
She's working hard.   It was developing rapidly.

State verbs can only be used with the progressive aspect under certain circumstances. The progressive is not normally used with verbs of perception, feeling, for relationships or states of being, except when the verb is used as an activity verb or for internal sensations.
I am seeing them tonight.   He is feeling tired.

- The Present Progressive is used for: a temporary event, a temporary habit, an almost certain intended future. It can also be used with an adverb of frequency to show annoyance: *He's always whistling!*
- The Past Progressive is used for: a temporary event or habit which is clearly identifiable as being in the past.

The Perfect aspect
Form This is formed with *has/have* + past participle.

The Present Perfect	*I have visited Rome.*
The Present Perfect Progressive	*I have been watching TV.*
The Past Perfect	*I had seen him before.*
The Past Perfect Progressive	*I had been sleeping earlier.*

Use   The perfect aspect is used to relate a past happening to another time:
They have been here before. So they are here now too.

It also can imply indefiniteness:
Have you read any Tolstoy?
(at any time in your life)
It is often found in conjunction with specific time adverbials, like *since* or *up to then.*
We have lived here since 1988. Up to then we had lived in Rome.

The future
The concept of futurity can be expressed in different ways.
1 Auxiliary verbs in combination with aspect:

with will/shall	*I will be there.*
with be going to	*I am going to leave.*
will/shall + progressive	*I will be finishing tomorrow.*
will/shall + perfect	*I will have finished by then.*
be going to + progressive	*I am going to be seeing him.*
be going to + perfect	*I am going to have finished.*

2 Using the following tenses:

Simple Present	*I leave tonight.*
Present Progressive	*I'm leaving tonight.*

3 Using the following verb phrases:

to be about to	*She is about to go away.*
to be to	*We are to consider it tomorrow.*
to be on the point of	*It's on the point of exploding.*
to be bound to	*He's bound to fail.*

Concepts and use Each of the above tenses indicates a particular concept of time. Many of these differences in concept are very subtle and the best way to understand the various uses is to study the verb phrase within each context.

Future in the Past

To express this concept there are three possibilities:

1 *She said she would do it.* (reporting of *will* intention)
2 *I was going to go but it proved impossible.* (unfulfilled intention)
3 *It was going to be difficult.* (past expectation)

Past in the Future

This concept can be expressed by:

- *will* + Present Perfect: *She will have finished by then.*
- *will* + Present Perfect Progressive: *He'll have been sleeping for 20 hours by then.*
- *will* + Present Progressive: *I'll be lying on the beach by 3.00 pm.*

The subjunctive

The subjunctive form of verbs in English is only occasionally used.

- The present form is the same as the stem of the verb:
  I propose that the motion be withdrawn.
- The past form is the same as the simple past (exception to be):
  It's time we left. If he were told, he'd be shocked.
- We use the subjunctive only:
1 in formal language
2 after specific verbs + *that* clause: *suggest, propose, demand, require, insist.*
  She proposed that he be excluded from the meeting.
3 with specific expressions:
  God/Allah be praised!   *I'd sooner go now.*
  It is time she understood.   *I'd rather he came.*

  If only it were me.   *I wish it were me.*
  Suppose we went too.
4 in conditionals (see page 180):
  If I were you, I'd try again.
  She walked in as if she owned the place.

Passive voice

There are two voices in English, the active and the passive. Most active sentences can be stated in the passive but they must have an object (a noun phrase or a pronoun).

Form

1 The passive voice is formed with the verb *to be* and can be used with all tenses and future forms. For example:
  a *A man was murdered last night.*
  b *This coat was made in Italy.*
  c *English will be spoken at all times.*
  d *As you know she has already been interviewed.*
  e *They will be given the award by the Director.*
2 Sometimes we can form the passive with the verb *to get.* This is an informal, spoken style and the agent is usually not given. For example:
  f *She got killed.*
  g *Nobody has got hurt yet.*
3 The agent (the subject of the sentence in the active), is often not stated because:
- it is not known (see *a, f*)
- it is irrelevant (see *b*)
- it has been clearly established in the context (*c, g*)
- it is understood because of common knowledge (*d*)

When there is no given agent we use common sense to supply one:
  passive: *Spanish is spoken all over the world.*
  active: *People speak Spanish all over the world.*

To transform a sentence from active to passive, or passive to active the object becomes the subject:

Active to passive: *Everybody sang the anthem.*
  becomes: *The anthem was sung (by everybody).*
Passive to active: *The flowers were made by children.*
  becomes: *Children made the flowers.*

Use We often use the passive in scientific and technical texts, reports, newspaper articles etc.

We can also use it to draw attention to a particular feature (see Emphasis, page 183).

Reported speech

Form When we report what someone said, we often, but not always, change the tense, pronominal reference and adverbials.

'I hate you.'	*She said (that) she hated him.*
'I'll be waiting for you.'	*He said he would be waiting for her.*
'Paul left yesterday.'	*I said Paul had left the day before.*

However it is not always necessary to change the tense, particularly if the information is still true:

'Her name's Jane.'	*I said her name's Jane.*

Time and place adverbials change in reported speech.

this morning/week	→ *that morning/week*
today	→ *that day*
tomorrow	→ *the day after*
ago	→ *before*
now	→ *then, at that moment*
here	→ *there*

Reporting verbs

Often we do not want to report what was said exactly word for word. Instead we summarise the content by using a reporting verb.

'I won't go,' she said.   *She refused to go.*

Some of the verbs which we can use in this way are: *agree, ask, complain, explain, order, persuade, tell, threaten, warn.*

Modal verbs

Modal verbs give information about the attitude, belief or feeling of the speaker. They are: *can, may, shall, will, could, might, should, would, must, ought to.*
The semi-modals are: *need, dare, used to.*

Form   Modal verbs do not have *-s* forms, *-ing* forms or *-ed* participles.
- They are usually followed by the stem of a main verb:
It might be possible.   *They should arrive soon.*
or by the perfect infinitive without *to*:
There may have been trouble.
The exception is *ought to*:
You ought to have helped.
- The negative is formed by adding *not* after the modal:
You cannot come.
- Some modals have limited time reference, and alternative verbs may be used. See *can.*

Meaning and use   Meaning is expressed both by choice of modal and by the way something is said. The modal alone gives a general indication. Each modal has a range of implied meanings.

can/could
- *Can* is used to indicate ability and inability, possibility and impossibility, permission and refusal, suggestion, offer, speculation.
- *Could* is used to express possibility and impossibility, suggestion, offer, speculation. We use *could* in the past, the conditional and in reported speech. It is also used to convey an unfulfilled ability or possibility.
- In general, when *can* and *could* are both possible, *could* is more polite or more tentative than *can.*
- *Could* is not used for ability or permission when referring to one particular action in the past. *To be able to* and *to be allowed to* are often used in this case. These forms are always used in the future, and are more formal than *can.*

may/might
- *May* and *might* are used to express permission, probability, possibility, offer, speculation.
- *Might* is used to replace *may* in reported speech, to express criticism or annoyance, to make a suggestion or a request. In general, *might* is considered more polite or more tentative. But in speech the intonation will give the real meaning.
- To express possible ability or possible necessity we can use *may/might* in a verb phrase with *be able to.*
- *May* and *might* usually refer to present and future. They can refer to the past by using the perfect infinitive.

shall
- *Shall* is used to express offers, suggestions, promises, threats, official decisions.
Shall we take our sandwiches with us?
I shall have that finished by this afternoon.
- In modern English *shall* is not used very frequently.
- *Shall* becomes *should* in reported speech.

will
- *Will* is used to convey either the notion of prediction or of volition. Prediction can be of general future, of present events, or expected habit.
It'll rain tomorrow.   *He'll be there by now.*
She will do that.

Volition can represent a promise or threat, personal intention, or willingness.
I'll get you later!   She will succeed.
He'll probably do it.
- It is also used in some conditionals (see page 180).

would

- *Would* is used to express future in the past, unfulfilled past, habitual past, past refusal, request, invitation, wish, willingness, evasion, annoyance, opinion.
- It is used as a past form of *will.*
- It is also used in conditionals (see page 180).

should

Should is used to express obligation, advice, warning, unfulfilled duty, expectations.
- It can be a past form for *shall* and replaces it in reported speech.
- Sometimes it is used to replace *would* in first and second persons.
- *Should* is also used in certain subordinate clauses:
    after *in case, so that, in order that*
    after certain verbs *suggest that, propose that*
    after *that* clauses following adjectives such as *sorry, shocked, interested*
    in conditionals showing increasing doubt.

ought to

- *Ought to* is used to express probability, obligation or advice, and is very similar in meaning to *should.*
- The negative is formed by placing *not* before *to.*
    You ought not to smoke so much.
- It may be used with the perfect infinitive to refer to the past.
    You ought to have spoken to her.

must

- *Must* is used to express obligation or speculation.
- It is only used for present and future. In past time use *to have to.*
    He must pay for the car.   He had to pay for the car.
- The negative form has the same meaning in present and future. But the past negative means *was not necessary.*

need

- *Need* expresses necessity, and as a modal it is generally only in negatives.
- It has no past tense form.
- It can also be used as a full verb, *to need.*

used to

- *Used to* expresses a past habit, usually not occurring at the moment of speaking. It only exists in the past form.
    When I was young, I used to play the piano.
- Forms for the interrogative and negative:
    Did she use to teach him?
    I didn't use to go. or *I used not to go.*
    NB   Do not confuse this modal with the verb *to be used to* meaning *to be accustomed to.*

dare

Dare expresses *not be afraid,* a challenge, a warning, an exclamation. It is not very often used nowadays, except in certain phrases. It can also be used as a full verb *to dare.*

Determiners

Determiners are used to identify particular nouns. The basic principle of countable versus uncountable nouns in singular and plural controls our choice of determiner.

Articles

The articles *the, a/an* or the zero article.
- *the* is used for all singular and plural countable nouns and uncountable nouns:
    the dog, the dogs, the milk
- *a/an* is used only for singular countable nouns: *a house, an apple*
- *zero article* is used for plural countable nouns and uncountable nouns: *dogs, milk*

Articles can be used to express the idea of 'in general'. There are three alternative ways of referring to *all/any:*
- zero article   (All) *Insects have six legs.*
- a/an   (Any) *An insect has six legs.*
- the   (All/Any) *The insect has six legs.*

Articles can be used to express general or particular:
- *a/an   Did you know she bought a horse?*
    (one of a kind, or a group - a horse in general)
- *the   She bought the horse in July.*
    (a specific horse we know about)

Other types of determiner

We can also determine nouns with the following:

this/that, these/those, every, each*, either*, neither*, both*, all*, some/any*, such (a), much, whichever/whatever.

- Singular countable nouns can use: *this/that, every, each, either, neither, any, such a, whichever/whatever.*
- Plural countable nouns can use: *these/those, both, all, some/any, such, whichever/whatever.*
- Uncountable nouns can use: *this/that, some/any, such, much, whichever/whatever.*

* These can be used with the *of* construction.
  Both of the books will help.
  All of the boys can come.
  Some of the wine was bad.
  Any of the clients were welcome.

Intensifiers

Intensifiers are words or phrases which give additional information. Most common intensifiers are adverbs but some are noun or prepositional phrases. They may qualify nouns, noun phrases, adjective phrases, adverbial phrases, and prepositional phrases. Many intensifiers precede the phrases but some follow them.

There is a basic division between absolute and gradable intensifiers.
- absolute intensifiers emphasise the total/whole:
  definitely, certainly, really, absolutely
- gradable intensifiers either increase, or decrease:
  increase: *very, much, so, a lot, well, a great deal, rather, quite*
  decrease: *sort of, quite, rather, a bit, partly, almost, nearly, hardly.*

When selecting an intensifier it is very important to consider the collocation very carefully. Think about the meaning of the item to be qualified and the meaning of the intensifier. Remember that some intensifiers can change their meaning eg. *rather, quite.*

Clauses

Relative clauses
Relative clauses follow the noun they describe.

There are more than two types: defining and non-defining. Defining clauses are essential to the meaning of the sentence because they identify who or what is being talked about. Non-defining clauses provide additional information.

Defining	Non-defining
cannot be omitted from sentence	can be omitted
no punctuation is necessary	commas are essential
common in spoken and written language	mostly in written language
no pauses in spoken language	clear pauses when spoken
formal and informal	mostly formal register

Defining
- Subject: we use *who/that* for people and *which/that* for things:
  Her friend who/that works here will meet us.
  The job which was advertised is still vacant.
- Object: we use *who/that* for people, *which/that* for things, *whose* for possession, *when* for time, *where* for place, and *why* for reason:
  There's the woman (*that) you saw before.
  Give me the book (*that) you bought.
  The man whose house we saw is very old.
  The time (*when) you want to go is not the best.
  The place (*where) you want to go is Rome.
  The reason (*why) he left is not known.

* In spoken language we often omit the relative pronoun (when it is the object). This is not possible with *whose*.

We can omit the relative pronoun and auxiliary verb to leave a noun phrase, but only when the pronoun relates to the subject.
  The animals which were living there were all killed.
  becomes: *The animals living there were all killed.*
  People who had been made homeless were given help.
  becomes: *People made homeless were given help.*

Non-defining
Both subject and object use *who* and *which*. We can also use *whom* (person) to define the object, but this is more formal. We can equally use *whose, when* and *where* when appropriate. Commas are used to separate the non-defining clause from the rest of the sentence.
  Peter, who phoned us earlier, will not be coming.
  The shark, which is a ferocious animal, attacks unexpectedly.

The naturalist, whose paper you read, will attend the meeting.
Pass it to me at a suitable time, when you have finished.
I visited the beach, where I found hundreds of jellyfish.

Prepositions in relative clauses

Nowadays we mostly place any prepositions at the end of the clause except in formal written register.
I gave it to the people I live with.
Here's the book which you looked at.
Placing prepositions before the pronoun is more common with non-defining clauses.
His article, to which you refer, is very concise.
The income, on which they rely, has been cut.

Clauses of reason

A clause explaining the reason for something may begin with any of the following conjunctions: *because, as, since, for.*
• *because* is the most common one. It usually follows the main clause. *She left her job because she hated it.*
• *as* and *since* usually precede the main clause. *As she had no more money she went home.*
Since her parents wouldn't help she came here.
• *For* is more unusual. It usually follows the main clause.
I helped her, for who else would help?

Clauses of purpose

Clauses of purpose can follow or precede the main clause. They are indicated by:
the infinitive with *to, in order to, so as to.*
She rang the company to ask for their address.
In order to finalise the deal they agreed to meet.
They took a taxi so as not to be late.
In formal language we can also use *in order that,* or *so that.*
The meeting was postponed in order that he could attend.
She translated it so that everyone could understand.
All the above can be formed into cleft sentences by using *it.* (See page 183).

Clauses of result

Clauses of result express the factual result of an action. The clause is introduced by *so that,* but *that* is often omitted in spoken or informal language.

I gave her a copy so (that) she knew about everything.
We can also use *such* + a noun phrase + *that.*
The conference was such a success that we will have another.
We cannot form cleft sentences with result clauses.

Noun clauses

There are four kinds of noun clause: *that* clause, *wh-* clause, infinitive clause and *-ing* clause

Noun clauses can replace or follow noun phrases. For example,
Nobody believes him. (noun phrase)
Nobody believes that he can do it. (*that* clause)
Nobody believes what he says. (*wh-* clause)
She asked us a question. (noun phrase)
She asked us to explain our reasons. (infinitive)
I don't mind their attitude. (noun phrase)
I don't mind them being aggressive. (*-ing* clause)
(noun phrase/*-ing*)
See also Emphasis page 183.

Conditionals

Conditionals consist of two clauses; one giving the condition, the other the result. In many cases the two clauses are not together but are given elsewhere in the discourse or understood from the context. The common conjunction is *if.* However, we also use: *unless, provided that, so long as, on condition that.*

Form

conditional	condition clause	result clause
zero	Simple Present	Simple Present
first	Simple Present	will + verb
second	Simple Past	would + verb
third	Past Perfect	would have + verb (-ed)
mixed	Past Perfect	would + verb

Use
• The zero conditional expresses certainty and fact:
If you mix green and yellow, you make blue.
• The first conditional expresses possibility:
If it rains, I'll go to the cinema.
• The second conditional expresses unlikely probability or an impossible hypothesis for speculation:
If I were you, I'd resign.

- The third conditional expresses a past impossible speculation.
  If he had been there, he would have seen her.
- The mixed conditional expresses impossibility with a past condition and a present result.
  If the car had been cleaned, I would be able to use it.

Other ways of expressing condition

There are a variety of alternative forms which operate as conditionals and sometimes indicate changes in meaning.
- modals can be used within either clause to change the likelihood:
  If I could go tonight, I might wear my pink shoes.
- *supposing: Supposing he doesn't arrive, what'll we do?*
- inversion: *Had I known he was going to be late, I'd have delayed dinner.*
- stressed auxiliaries: *If he did miss the train, he would've phoned.*

Wishes/regrets

The verb *to wish* is followed by a variety of clauses similar to conditionals. It is used to express:
- impossible speculation: a wish (state and event verbs)
  I wish I were you.
- possible speculation: a wish (event verbs only)
  I wish he wouldn't do that.
- impossible past speculation: a regret (state and event verbs)
  I wish I had known.

If only can be used instead of *to wish*: *If only I had known.* See also Subjunctive p 176.

Comparison, Similarity and Preference

Comparatives

...er/more than

We use *...er* and *more than* with adjectives and adverbs to compare two items.
We use *-er* with
- one-syllable adjectives and adverbs:
  His report was longer than hers.
  She drives faster in her new car.
- some two syllable adjectives
  Can you get out? The gap is narrower than before.

We use *more* with
- two or more syllable adverbs:
  He gave it up more happily than I thought.
- some two syllable adjectives:
  It was also more complex.
- all adjectives with three or more syllables:
  This is more expensive than the other shop.

Superlatives

the ...est/most

The superlative of adjectives follows the same rules as for comparatives:
  That is the oldest piece I have seen.
  It is the loveliest painting.
  She is the most capable person for this job.
Most adverbs use the *most* form:
  It is the most easily understood.
Exceptions are: *fast, hard, early, late, long, near, soon, well, and far :*
  She works the hardest.

Equality

as ... as

As ... as is used with adjectives, adverbs, *much/ many*, or nouns preceded by *much/many*.
  Jane is as tall as Mary. Paul drives as well as Angela.
  You ate as many chocolates as I did.
  She earns as much money as before.

not as/so ... as

To negate equality either *as* or *so* are used after the *not*.
  Jane is not so tall as Mary.
  Paul does not drive as well as Angela.
  You did not eat as many chocolates as I did.
  She does not earn so much money now.

as + prepositional/noun phrase

This is used as a subsidiary clause to give an example. Commas are used around the clause.
Exactly or *just* can precede the *as.*
  In 1986, (just) as in 1982, he won the election.
  She questioned him, as the officer had done, in French.

(in) the same way and the same as

Exactly or *just* can precede the expressions.
  You have to do it in exactly the same way.
  He did the same as last time.
If you use *almost* to qualify the expression then you express close similarity.
  That is almost the same as the other one.

like

This can be followed by a noun: *She looks just like her father.* Or a pronoun: *The photo really is not like her.*

alike

This means two items are similar to each other. It occurs at the end of a clause.

The two teams are very (much) alike.
Because they are alike, they get on very well.

similar to

This is followed by a noun/noun phrase, a pronoun, an adjective or a clause.

His coat is similar to mine.
The colour is similar to blue.
That is similar to what I said.

likewise

This means the same or in a similar way. It occurs at the end of a sentence following a verb.

I gave up the race, he did likewise.

as if/though

This is often used after the verbs *to seem* and *to appear*. The comparison may be real:

You look/appear as if you need a rest.
She sounded as though she were exhausted.

or it may be unreal:

It seemed as if it were going to rain (but it didn't).
He ran as though ghosts were chasing him.

See also Subjunctive page 176.

Difference

different from

This is the opposite of *similar to*. It is followed by a noun, noun phrase, pronoun or a clause.

His flat is different from the last one.

apart from

This means *except for* or *aside from*. It is followed by a noun or a noun phrase.

Apart from looking after the children, she has nothing to do.

otherwise

This is the opposite of likewise and means the opposite/alternative.

You do that then, I'll do otherwise.

other than

This means *different*. It is followed by a noun phrase or pronoun.

She needs help other than mine.

Preference

would rather/sooner

This means *would prefer*. It is followed by the infinitive without *to*:

I'd rather have this one (than that one).
Would you rather take the train or the boat?

When the preference is expressed about another person's action the following verb is in the past subjunctive:

I'd sooner you left.
He'd rather I were here.

See also Subjunctive page 176.

to prefer to

We use either the infinitive or the *-ing* form after prefer.

• The infinitive expresses specific instances:
  I'd prefer to travel by car to Granny's.
• The -ing form expresses general preferences:
  When you were young, did you prefer swimming or sailing?
  She prefers staying in to going out. (note the position of to)

Past preference

We use either *would rather* or *to prefer* depending on whether the event occurred (*a* and *b*) or not (*c* and *d*). The preference can be either for the speaker (*a* and *c*) or for someone else (*b* and *d*).

a He preferred to go.
b He preferred her to go.
c He would rather have gone.
d He would rather (that) she had gone.

Degree

enough

• This is used:
  after adjectives and adverbs:
  It was good enough for him. She sang well enough to win.
  or before nouns or *of* + a noun phrase
  I don't have enough help. She's had enough (of these) rumours.
• It can also be followed by the infinitive:
  She was kind enough to buy me one.
  or after verbs: *Do you eat enough?*
• But it only follows the verb *to be* when the subject is a pronoun:
  That's enough.

too

This can be used:
• before an adjective: *It is too heavy.*
• before an adverb: *She drives too fast.*

- followed by the infinitive with to: *She is too slow to include.*
- with or without *for* + object: *It is too difficult for him to do.*
- combined with *much* it can follow a verb:
  You took too much money. You smoke too much.

the more/the less
- *The more/the less* compares the degree/amount between two items. The two clauses can be used in different combinations.
  The more you do the more you get.
  The less you do the less you get.
  The more you spend the less you have.
- We also use *the more/the less* with other adjectives in the comparative form.
  The quicker you are the better.
  The harder it is the slower he works.
  The sooner you go the happier I'll be.

Emphasis

In order to emphasise particular pieces of information we can use different techniques. The following are some of the most common.

Using initial sentence position
- *Having* + past participle:
  Having studied the report, she returned it.
- Past participle:
  Pleased with the result, he stopped.
- Infinitive:
  To thank everyone concerned, he ordered some champagne.
- Prepositional phrases, adverbial phrases and conjunctions:
  Under the tree, it lay for centuries.
  Yet it seems to be a very difficult situation.

(note the comma in the examples)
This is not a complete list. Other prepositions, adverbs and conjunctions can also be placed at the beginning of a sentence.

Inversion
We use interrogative word order (inversion) for emphasis:
- after certain adverbials which have a negative connotation: *never, hardly, scarcely, rarely, under no circumstances.*
  Never have I seen such a bad play.
  Rarely does he ever help.
- after expressions using *only:*

  Not only did I complain, but I also wrote to the newspaper.
- after *neither, nor* or *so:*
  Neither do I. Nor has she.
- in exclamations:
  Aren't you clever! Isn't he cute!

Cleft sentences
A common way of emphasising is by using the structures:
- *It is/was ... that...* to emphasise most parts of the sentence.
  Jane gave a report to the group.
  It was Jane who gave a report to the group.
  It was a report that Jane gave to the group.
  It was to the group that Jane gave a report.
- *What ... is/was...* to emphasise the subject or object.
  She saw what was her own work.
  What she saw was her own work.
  His attitude hurts. What hurts is his attitude.

Stressed auxiliaries
Inserting the relevant auxiliary verb in an affirmative structure gives emphasis and/or provides contrast. The auxiliary is stressed.
- the auxiliary depends on the tense of the main verb.
  I do think that is a good idea.
  That's not true, she did go.
  She will make so much noise.
- when the affirmative structure already uses an auxiliary, it is not contracted and it is stressed (strong form not weak form).
  I was very pleased.
  You have worked hard.

Vocabulary

Compound words
These are items of vocabulary made up of more than one word. The meaning is understood from the meaning of the parts. For example, a car has many parts: the windows, doors, wheels, etc. We can form the following compounds: *car seat, car door, car wheel.*

Compound words may be made of:
- two words: *oil well.*
- two joined words: *handshake.*
- two hyphenated words: *house-boat.*
There are no fixed rules for writing these, so check in a dictionary.

Compound words can be:
- nouns: *steam train* from *a train powered by steam*
- adjectives: *blue-eyed* from *with eyes which are blue*
- verbs: *to horseride* from *to ride on a horse*

They can be formed from phrasal verbs as in:

to hand out	*He handed out the books to the class.*
a handout	*He gave them handouts before the class.*

NB There is often a slight change in meaning.

They can also be formed with *-ing* or *-ed* adjectives:

boiling point   tortured mind
light-hearted manner

Phrasal verbs and prepositional verbs (multi-word verbs)

Verbs + adverbial particles are phrasal verbs:
EEC stands for European Economic Community.
Verbs with a preposition and following phrase are prepositional verbs: *She stood on the top step.*
Some multi-word verbs take both adverbial particle and preposition:
She really looked up to her mother.

In structural terms there are four types of multi-word verbs.

type	object	position of object	position	passive
1 *to come across*	yes	after	phrase	yes
2 *to catch up*	no	–	–	no
3 *to bring up*	yes	nouns before and after; pronouns before	–	yes
4 *to fall back on*	yes	after	–	yes

Type 1: *I came across them when I was looking for my book.*
Type 2: *He didn't study last year and he has never caught up.*
Type 3: *He brought them/the children up extremely well.*
He brought up the children extremely well.
Type 4: *The tragedy forced her to fall back on herself.*

Suffixes and prefixes

These are additions made to change the meaning of words. Prefixes are added to the beginning of a word, suffixes to the end. Each prefix and suffix has a particular meaning. Some examples are:

prefix	meaning	example
inter-	between	international
pre-	before	prefix
sub-	under/lower	subway

suffix	meaning	example
-ette	compact/small	cigarette
-ish	somewhat	reddish
-less	without	restless

Synonyms and antonyms

A synonym is a word which has the same meaning as another. An antonym has the opposite meaning. For example, *to increase/to raise* versus *to decrease/to lower*